THE SOTL GUIDE

Open Access Book Series

The **Center for Engaged Learning** (CEL) Open Access Book Series features concise, peer-reviewed books and edited collections for a multi-disciplinary, international, higher education audience interested in research-informed engaged learning practices. CEL is committed to making these publications freely available to a global audience. *Series editors, Jessie L. Moore and Peter Felten*

Select Publications

Inclusive Pedaoggy in Practice: Perspectives from Equity-Minded College Educators
Edited by Amelia Koford, Corinne Castro, and Christopher Bollinger
doi.org/10.36284/celelon.oa9

Counterstory Pedagogy: Student Letters of Resilience, Healing, and Resistance
Edited by Adriana Aldana
doi.org/10.36284/celelon.oa8

Online, Open, and Equitable Education: Lessons from Teaching and Learning during the Global Pandemic
Edited by Nancy K. Turner, Nick Baker, David J. Hornsby, Aline Germain-Rutherford, David Graham, and Brad Wuetherick
doi.org/10.36284/celelon.oa7

Becoming a SoTL Scholar
Edited by Janice Miller-Young and Nancy Chick
doi.org/10.36284/celelon.oa6

Writing Beyond the University: Preparing Lifelong Learners for Lifewide Writing
Edited by Julia Bleakney, Jessie L. Moore, and Paula Rosinski
doi.org/10.36284/celelon.oa5

What Teaching Looks Like: Higher Education through Photographs
Cassandra Volpe Horii and Martin Springborg
doi.org/10.36284/celelon.oa4

The SoTL Guide

(Re)Orienting the Scholarship of Teaching and Learning

Nancy L. Chick, Peter Felten, and Katarina Mårtensson

Center for Engaged Learning at Elon University
Elon, North Carolina

Parlor Press
Anderson, South Carolina

Center for Engaged Learning at Elon University
Elon, North Carolina
www.CenterForEngagedLearning.org

Series editors: Jessie L. Moore and Peter Felten
Copyeditor and designer: Sophie Grabiec

©2025 by Nancy L. Chick, Peter Felten, and Katarina Mårtensson. This work is made available under a Creative Commons Attribution-NonCommercial-NoDerivatives 4.0 International license.

The current edition is distributed and sold by Parlor Press with these ISBNs:
ISBN (PBK) 978-1-64317-567-6
ISBN (PDF) 978-1-64317-568-3
ISBN (EPUB) 978-1-64317-569-0

Library of Congress Cataloging-in-Publication Data
Names: Nancy L. Chick, Peter Felten, and Katarina Mårtensson
Title: The SoTL Guide: (Re)Orienting the Scholarship of Teaching and Learning/ Nancy L. Chick, Peter Felten, and Katarina Mårtensson
Description: Elon, North Carolina : Elon University Center for Engaged Learning, 2025 | Series: Center for engaged learning open access book series | Includes bibliographical references and index.
Identifiers: ISBN (PDF) 978-1-64317-568-3 ISBN (PBK) 978-1-64317-567-6 ISBN (EPUB) 978-1-64317-569-0 | DOI https://doi.org/10.36284/celelon.oa10
Subjects: Education, Higher—Research | College teaching
Classification: LCC LB2331 .C45 2025 | DDC 378.125

CONTENTS

Introduction	1
Section 1: Getting Oriented	8
Why SoTL?	9
Why You?	25
Section 2: Taking the Journey	43
SoTL Entry Points	44
Meaningful SoTL Questions	70
Situating Your Work in SoTL Conversations	86
Relational SoTL Ethics	107
Designing Your Inquiry	120
Collecting "Traces of Learning"	135
Analyzing Artifacts Systematically	151
Sharing What You Learn	165
Section 3: Looking Ahead	187
For You as an Individual	188
For You in a Community of Scholars	205
References	223
Index	256

Acknowledgments

We are grateful to so many colleagues who've informed our thinking about SoTL over the years. We also appreciate those who provided feedback on our draft. The anonymous reviewers were thorough, constructive, and specific, and Johan Geertsema, who generously volunteered to provide feedback, offered precisely the kind of encouragement, insight, and complementary thinking we've come to appreciate about SoTL colleagues.

We also must thank two colleagues from the Center for Engaged Learning: Sophie Grabiec, managing editor, and Jessie Moore, Open Access series editor. We can't imagine more supportive, competent, and understanding editors.

Introduction

Welcome to *The SoTL Guide!* We're glad you're here. Before we get to the Scholarship of Teaching and Learning (SoTL), let us tell you about ourselves and how we came to write this book. The three of us—Nancy, Peter, and Katarina—met through SoTL. We started by admiring each other's work. That appreciation *for the work* led to conversations and collaborations with each other *as people*, which then led to even more admiration. Over time, we came to know and enjoy each other beyond our professional selves. We decided to write this book because we knew we wanted to share our experiences and insights from the work each of us has done with SoTL, and to capture the humanness that we (and others) bring to that work and that this work elevates in us.

We also wrote this book because we have a vision for SoTL to be an even more positive force in higher education—for those of us who teach and work in academia, for our students, and for our communities. Our definition of SoTL may be simple (see "What Is SoTL?" in chapter 1), but our vision for SoTL is ambitious. We see SoTL as more than one thing: it's a practice that improves teaching and learning in context. It's also a field that extends how

> **BOX 0.1**
>
> **A Simple Definition**
>
> In chapter 1, we define SoTL as: inquiry into teaching and learning for the purposes of improving teaching and learning in context and contributing to what we know about teaching and learning, in support of the broader aims of higher education.

we in higher education build knowledge. It's a community that offers rich relationships for those who seek them. And it's a form of scholarship with socially conscious and humane roots that call on us to make a difference in the education of students, in the careers of academics, and in the world.

We see so much promise in SoTL. This orientation towards our work in and on SoTL and to each other also shapes how we wrote this book. We chose to write *The SoTL Guide* by simultaneously embracing and resisting a stepwise approach to doing SoTL. Like the other helpful books on developing SoTL inquiries, we appreciate making the inquiry process more transparent and accessible. Unpacking the unfamiliar and identifying key steps makes SoTL a more welcoming, inclusive, and effective field. At the same time, we've seen how some of the best SoTL inquiries result from the willingness to follow what emerges, to welcome surprises, and to change direction. We hope the book's approach to developing a SoTL inquiry reflects this structured flexibility.

Stylistically, we chose to write the book in an inviting and often informal voice (and occasionally, voices) because we've experienced SoTL as a collegial practice—a form of scholarly conversation among peers who come from different backgrounds and contexts and who come together to understand each other, to draw out and complement each other's strengths, and ultimately to strive toward shared goals in tackling complex issues in higher education.

Also, as we bring in these peers, we're intentionally adopting an approach that recognizes not only the products of their work (i.e., their publications) but also the effort and humanness that led to these products. It's too easy to reduce our peers to an article, a conclusion, even a disembodied PDF on a screen, and we want to uplift the very human work of our colleagues, especially in the wake of generative AI tools. Our approach may feel unfamiliar as you read *The SoTL Guide*, but we invite you to pause during those moments to consider what we're attempting to highlight, and why. For instance, when we write about specific SoTL inquiries, our attribution includes something about the people and their work that we see as important. We want to signal that *who is doing the work* and *where they are doing it* matter. To capture this information, we first must name the people. We include the authors' full names—or, in a few cases of unpublished inquiries, the full names of those who conducted the project. We occasionally depart from the *Chicago Manual of Style*'s guidelines by including all of the authors' names, rather than using *et al.* (For more on this approach to citation, see "Naming Is Power: Citation Practices in SoTL" by Chick, Ostrowdun, Abbot, Mercer-Mapstone, and Grensavitch [2021].) We also note the contexts for their inquiries—typically the geographical region, the general type of institution, the discipline or course, and the year. Far more about context matters to each SoTL project, but in the end we decided that this information will help readers meaningfully situate each project and see all projects as meaningfully situated. In some chapters, you'll also see that we center specific scholars whose thinking has deeply informed the overarching guidance of that chapter, so in these instances we briefly describe those scholars' roles and contexts that are relevant to that influence. And sometimes we simply name authors who we draw on to make a small but significant point. We invite you to try this approach to citing in your own work; we see this as one way to extend the interpersonal generosity of the SoTL community into our scholarly practice.

We also include many voices beyond our own throughout the book. Some writerly conventions urge us to summarize and paraphrase outside sources as much as possible, but that can also feel like an act of erasure. Writing is difficult, and the craft of putting together effective words, phrases, and sentences is part of the influential work we want to honor, so in parts of this book, you'll see more direct quotations here than you see in some other texts. That isn't lazy writing; it's collegial writing.

You may also notice that we feature colleagues from a range of disciplines, institutions, nationalities, and identities, representing some of the diversity of those who practice SoTL. Admittedly, we depict only some of that diversity, and we surely depict it incompletely. For instance, nearly all of our citations are from English-language sources, which says more about us as authors (i.e., Katarina is multilingual, but Nancy and Peter are fluent only in English, so our joint language is English) than SoTL itself, which is certainly happening in plenty of languages, as we show in chapter 1.

Our ongoing, imperfect efforts to represent the diversity of the field illustrate how the SoTL we present in this book reflects not only what we have learned, but—more importantly—what we continue to learn. Writing this book together was a journey of discovery for each of us, and we know that we haven't always lived up to the SoTL we describe in the following pages, but we believe there's great value in articulating our shared aspirations. Writing *The SoTL Guide* has been, in some ways, as much a guide for us as we hope it will be for you. We hope you'll find the ideas, the examples, the frameworks, and the questions in *The SoTL Guide* to be both practical and inspiring, both informational and aspirational.

We initially conceived of *The SoTL Guide* as a book for readers who are relatively new to SoTL, but in the same way that we learned so much from each other through this collaborative writing, we realized that more experienced scholars will find things that surprise and even challenge them in these pages. And since we have the dual role of SoTL practitioners and SoTL supporters, we also believe that academic developers will be able to adapt materials from the book in their programming (see box 0.2).

To ease your navigation on this journey, we divided *The SoTL Guide* into three sections:

- **Getting Oriented:** In the first section (chapters 1–2), we consider what SoTL is and who you are as a SoTL scholar.
- **Taking the Journey:** In the second section (chapters 3–10), we explore the process of developing a SoTL inquiry, focusing on frameworks and concepts that will help you as your work unfolds.
- **Looking Ahead:** In the third and final section (chapters 11–12), we dig into the implications of SoTL for you as a professional and as part of a community.

If you're new to SoTL, we encourage you to start at the beginning and read the chapters sequentially. If you're not new, we invite you to read in this way as well because we think we're offering something new in the book, and our approach to

SoTL—conceptualizing the field, designing a project, and situating yourself as a scholar—builds on that foundation.

We introduced ourselves and the book by noting how we met each other as peers and professionals and then, through conversation and collaboration, came to know and appreciate each other as people. Throughout this book, then, when we refer to SoTL as a scholarly conversation, we're not simply invoking a useful metaphor. Our relationships with each other—and with many other colleagues, collaborators, and friends in SoTL—developed through conversations. We mean it when we say that we hope *The SoTL Guide* inspires you not only to develop SoTL inquiries but also to join SoTL conversations and build this community. When we inquire on our own, SoTL can help us improve our teaching, but together SoTL can help us transform higher education.

BOX 0.2

A Note for Academic Developers Reading *The SoTL Guide*

We wrote *The SoTL Guide* directly for SoTL practitioners, or those who develop and conduct SoTL projects, but we can also imagine it being used as a valuable resource in academic development. As all three of us are engaged in academic development in our respective institutions (as well as nationally and internationally) we've shared our understanding of SoTL, how to develop SoTL inquiries, and a variety of activities and tools just as we've done in workshops with academic teachers from many contexts. We hope the book is both practical and inspiring for academic developers.

Since the book and its supplemental materials are open access and freely available, we invite you to use the whole book or parts of it as it fits your context. Our approach will support your engagement of colleagues who are either new to or experienced with SoTL. A few possibilities, for example, are below:

- Each section or chapter can be a stand-alone topic for workshops and conversations. The guidance, explanations, and reflective questions (which can alternatively be used as discussion questions) may provide all you need to facilitate a discussion or organize a workshop.
- Some or all of the book can be used to support an in-person or virtual SoTL program or learning community. Participants might read one chapter at a time (or just the chapters that are relevant to your focus), and then share their reflections and responses to the "Questions for You" at the end of each chapter. We can see this approach supporting the "significant conversations" that nurture changes in practice and the development of lasting collegial relationships (Roxå and Mårtensson 2009, 556).
- We also encourage you to be creative in how you use the book in your specific context.

After you use the book—in parts or as a whole, on your own or with your colleagues—we would be eager to hear from you to learn how you used it, how it went, and any other feedback you'd be willing to share.

SECTION 1

Getting Oriented

CHAPTER 1

Why SoTL?

"More poignantly, I realized that the cycle of scholarly teaching and learning is ongoing and that none of us can claim to have ever 'arrived.'"
—Kasturi Behari-Leak (2020)

In the quote above, Kasturi Behari-Leak relates some of what she learned about the Scholarship of Teaching and Learning (SoTL) at the 2019 conference of the International Society for the Scholarship of Teaching and Learning (ISSOTL). A researcher in higher education and a high-profile academic developer in South Africa, she felt "trepidation and excitement" when she arrived at the conference (2020, 4), even though she was going to be the opening keynote speaker. She was excited because the year's theme of borders and social justice resonated deeply with her, but she was hesitant because it was her first ISSOTL conference, and she wondered, "Why me?" (2020, 4). After the conference, she describes coming to understand SoTL differently, as a way "to unlearn, relearn, and reframe assumptions and practices" (2020, 5). In chapter 2, we will return to Behari-Leak's explicit question of "Why me?" by helping you explore why *you* may choose to do SoTL. But let's start with her broader yet implicit question, "Why SoTL?" To answer both of these questions, we'll need to establish what we mean by "SoTL."

What Is SoTL?

Good question! Put simply, we see SoTL as *inquiry into teaching and learning for the purposes of improving teaching and learning in context and contributing to what we know about teaching and learning, in support of the broader aims of higher education.* We know our definition is missing a lot of nuance. Indeed, some scholars have even devoted entire articles to this question, wrestling with different words and phrases and trying to distinguish SoTL from other activities. (On the book site, we offer a few of those definitional articles.) Rather than attempting to pin down a perfect definition at this point in our journey, we think a more helpful starting place is found in the commentary by some founders of the field chronicled in "Key Characteristics of SoTL," a video produced by Elon University's Center for Engaged Learning for the 2013 conference of the International Society for the Scholarship of Teaching and Learning. Listen carefully for what the interviewees describe as SoTL's key characteristics and common themes. According to this video, what does SoTL look like? What's its focus? How's it done? Who does it? For what purpose?

Although some disciplines have long researched how students learn in their courses, Ernest Boyer invited academic teachers (the term we'll use for *faculty, instructor, academic, tutor, academic staff, lecturer,* and variations on *professor*) from all disciplines to do this work when he coined the term "the scholarship of teaching" in his 1990 book *Scholarship Reconsidered*. (Soon after, "and learning" was added to Boyer's phrase, leading to "SoTL.") A leading voice in setting the national agenda for education in America, in part through his roles as President of the Carnegie Foundation for the Advancement of Teaching and then the head of the US Department of Education, Boyer described an urgent need to "break out of the tired old teaching versus research debate and define, in more creative ways, what it means to be a scholar" (1990, xii). Yes, Boyer was advocating for expanding how academic teachers get rewarded and promoted, but that wasn't his ultimate goal. Instead, he framed his call for change with greater significance: "[if] higher learning institutions are to meet today's urgent academic and social mandates, their missions must be carefully redefined and the meaning of scholarship creatively reconsidered" (1990, 13). The purpose of scholarship, research, and the other work grounded in disciplinary expertise is, according to Boyer, inextricable from the purpose of education. In an earlier book that previewed his attention to "today's urgent academic and social mandates," he argued that higher education's purpose is:

> not only to prepare students for productive careers but also to enable them to live lives of dignity and purpose; not only to generate new knowledge but also to channel that knowledge to humane ends; not merely to study government but to help shape a citizenry that can promote the public good. (Boyer 1987, 119)

In this way, the origin of SoTL as a multidisciplinary field is rooted in the claim that our "vision" about higher education more broadly and the specific pursuits of academics' scholarly work "must be widened if the [world] is to be rescued from problems that threaten to diminish permanently the quality of life" (1987, 119). Boyer's expansive and humane view embraces both important disciplinary objectives and broader "mandates" to contribute to more just and sustainable communities, in part by preparing students to do the same. Woven throughout Boyer's work, this clarion call recognizes the potential for SoTL to be transformational for academics, students, institutions, and communities. Today, some four decades later, this vision seems as important as ever.

Regardless of your motives right now, Boyer's reimagining of what it means to be a scholar is a helpful invitation—and challenge—to be mindful of the significance of teaching and learning in higher education. The work we do matters immensely for our students and our world, so we need to do it well. This is precisely why SoTL matters. By applying a scholarly lens to our teaching and our students' learning, SoTL enables us to better understand and systematically enhance what we do in higher education.

What does it mean to apply a scholarly lens to our teaching and to our students' learning? This question is part of the definitional discourse in SoTL (see our definition above and others in this chapter's supplemental materials), but a basic set of benchmarks is embedded in SoTL's characteristic of "going public." For this work to be "scholarship," as Boyer called it, our SoTL projects need to be open to peer review and feedback and contribute to scholarly knowledge beyond our self. In a frequently cited analysis, Lee S. Shulman, an American educational psychologist who followed Boyer as the President of the Carnegie Foundation for the Advancement of Teaching, distinguishes SoTL from scholarly teaching, which he says "every one of us should be engaged in every day … [in] all the roles we play pedagogically" (Shulman 2004, 166). To Shulman, scholarly teaching becomes SoTL the moment "we step back and reflect systematically on the teaching we have done, in a form that can be publicly reviewed and built upon by our peers" (2004, 166). As you'll see in chapter 9, the scope, scale, and form of the peer review and knowledge contribution vary, but this requirement is rooted in SoTL's origin. SoTL begins with an intention to contribute to something beyond ourselves. Throughout *The SoTL Guide*, you'll see this ethos of generosity in every step of developing a SoTL project. At the same time, we also know that, even among ourselves, there are many answers to the question, "Why SoTL?" Our next section will explore some of these answers.

"SoTL" in Translation

Obviously, this book—like much of SoTL—is written in English. Kasturi Behari-Leak notes that most of the research in the world is written in English and for English-speaking countries, a fact that "establishes linguistic borders that keep speakers of other languages out" (Behari-Leak 2020, 11). As an international field, SoTL struggles with this exclusivity based on language. Even beyond the confusion about, for instance, what to call people who teach at the postsecondary level or how to describe different types of educational institutions, the term "the scholarship of teaching and learning" has no direct translation in many places where English is not the primary language. In such contexts, people engaged in SoTL try to find other ways to express this work in their language.

Consider the European context, for example, where more than forty-five different languages are spoken. In Swedish, the most common translation of SoTL is "ett vetenskapligt förhållningssätt till undervisning," which in English means "a scientific approach to teaching and learning." German translations include "forschungsbasierte Auseinandersetzung mit der Lehre" ("research-based discussion of teaching and learning") and "strukturierte und systematische Erkundung von Aspekten der eigenen hochschulischen Lehre bzw. des studentischen Lernens (oder anderer damit verbundener Aspekte)" ("structured and systematic exploration of aspects of one's own teaching in higher education or of student learning [or other associated aspects]"), and in Spanish, it's "Enfoque Académico de la Enseñanza y el Aprendizaje" ("academic approach to teaching and learning").

These linguistic variations occur around the world. In Chinese, as used by some Taiwanese scholars, SoTL is expressed as "教與學的學術研究," which literally means "teaching and learning academic investigation." We could go on, but we trust you see our point.

These translations suggest some subtle differences, especially in the explication of "scholarship." Indeed, the word "scholarship" does not sit well with everyone in the English-speaking SoTL community; some prefer the term "research" or "inquiry" to describe what, in translation, is described as "a scientific approach," "research-based discussion," "structured and systematic exploration," "academic approach," and "academic investigation." Regardless of these differences and the challenges of the term, all share a core meaning that points to a scholarly, systematic approach to exploring teaching and learning.

We want to acknowledge this language complexity and the challenges of translating SoTL into other contexts—in part because context matters to SoTL, in part because we're keenly aware of the power of language described by Behari-Leak, and in part because our conversations in writing this book often gravitated to language. Given our varied language backgrounds—English as a first language for Nancy and Peter, and a second for Katarina—our communication is inevitably shaped by these linguistic differences.

BOX 1.1

SOTL AND EDUCATIONAL RESEARCH

You may be wondering, "Isn't SoTL just another name for educational research? And if it is, how can I possibly do SoTL if I'm not trained as an educational researcher?" We encourage you to think about SoTL and educational research as complementary but distinct. SoTL's primary focus is on specific students in a specific postsecondary teaching context, and a SoTL inquiry is typically conducted by the academic teacher in that context who is interested in—at the very least—improving learning and teaching in that context. SoTL often draws on an academic teacher's disciplinary expertise, meaning that SoTL is characterized by "disciplinary styles" that emerge from the research traditions of a wide range of fields (Huber and Morreale 2002).

In other words, SoTL practitioners do SoTL *at least in part* to improve their teaching and their students' learning, and they typically use their disciplinary training to pursue that inquiry. On the other hand, educational research is often more broadly focused on educational issues at all school levels, especially the years before students reach university, with a primary aim to add to existing knowledge about education and its conditions, using established methods in that particular field (Larsson, Mårtensson, Price, and Roxå 2020). Discipline-based education research (or DBER) is a specific type of educational research that focuses on learning and teaching in science and engineering (Fisher 2024; Singer, Nielsen, and Schweingruber 2012). While SoTL overlaps with educational research and DBER, SoTL is practiced by academic teachers in all disciplines and is interested in particularities, and educational research and DBER are practiced within a specific scholarly field and prioritizes generalization.

Many Reasons to Do SoTL

In this section, we explore some of the reasons why academic teachers begin doing SoTL and ultimately why many commit to this work. Some want to improve their teaching or students' learning. Others want to change their institutional environment or the profession of teaching. Still others want to contribute to the public good.

Below, we present these motivations as distinct, but we see them as interrelated (see figure 1.1, next page). Doing SoTL makes us better at what we do, and it resonates outward to influence our students, our institutional culture, our profession, and even the world beyond higher education, in line with what Boyer intended. Also, when we first engage with SoTL or when we begin any given SoTL project, we may focus on just one or two of these reasons. On a pragmatic and day-to-day level, we might not aim as high as Boyer, but these ripples illustrate some of the indirect and ultimate outcomes of SoTL. Just as we often don't know about our impact on our students until they reach out with gratitude years later, so too are we unaware of some of the consequences of our SoTL work. This framework suggests that scholarly inquiry into teaching and learning may have ripple effects beyond our initial intentions.

Teaching

Many of us come to SoTL to improve our teaching practice. Most academics were mainly trained to do research, and teaching is something we often learn by doing, imitating the teachers we appreciated or avoiding becoming like those we didn't. We may have the opportunity to take part in professional development activities to learn about teaching, or perhaps we find an

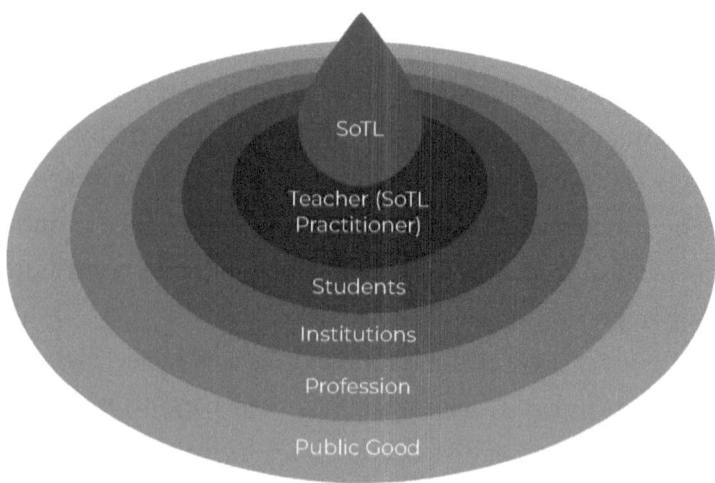

Figure 1.1. Many reasons for doing SoTL, showing how individual motivations for inquiry ripple outward to impact students, institutions, disciplines, and society.

experienced colleague to be our mentor. But how we learn to teach—and continue learning to teach *well*—is often informal and episodic. This is a common reason why many of us engage in SoTL: We want to feel less like an "amateur in the operating room," to borrow David Pace's memorable phrase about teaching in his discipline of history (Pace 2004, 1171). We want to refine and improve our teaching, or "[find] new vocabulary to describe [our] challenges and innovation" (Samuel 2017, 22). This goal may begin with something simple like hoping to learn how to facilitate group work more effectively, improve our assessment techniques, or motivate students to read.

Over time, this goal may evolve into changing our entire approach to teaching, or our understanding of its purpose, how it's done well, and how it's connected to learning. In his research on how academic teachers conceive of teaching and learning, Keith Trigwell found that those who do SoTL also tend to report what he calls a Conceptual Change/Student-Focused approach and facilitate activities to "provoke discussion and debate, monitor students' changing understanding, and encourage students to question their own ideas" (Trigwell 2013, 98). This teaching philosophy adopted by many SoTL practitioners contrasts with the Information Transmission/Teacher-Focused [ITTF] approach that views teaching as a one-way transfer of knowledge, skills, and facts through "good presentation, covering the content, and providing a good set of notes" (Trigwell 2013, 98). In earlier research, Trigwell and Michael Prosser found that this Conceptual Change/Student-Focused approach and its accompanying teaching practices are likely to transform students' fundamental understanding of whatever they're studying and perhaps even their entire world view (Trigwell and Prosser 1996). As we engage with SoTL, as suggested by this research, our understanding of our roles as teachers starts to align more with Boyer's broader vision.

Student Learning

We teach so that students learn, so some of us come to SoTL to better understand how that learning happens, the conditions that best support learning, and the experiences of our students as they learn. In SoTL, what we mean by *learning* is intentionally broad, an expansive view that spans from acquiring knowledge and building skills to developing minds, habits, capacities, and values. The cognitive processes we often associate with learning (e.g., concept comprehension and application, disciplinary ways of knowing, skill development, memory and transfer) occur in a larger realm of relationships and identities that inform these activities. SoTL's lens on student learning is panoramic. For example, much research about learning in recent decades has

BOX 1.2

Students as Partners

A powerful extension of SoTL's focus on the entire learning *experience* is collaborating with students as partners in SoTL inquiries. In this practice, students aren't simply viewed as the learners being studied: they are also co-inquirers who bring their perspectives and expertise as learners to SoTL inquiries. These partnerships have the potential to be transformative for SoTL inquiries and for the people doing those inquiries. At the same time, this kind of co-inquiry challenges many of the hierarchical customs and habits of higher education. To explore examples of partnership, you might start by browsing these three open access resources:
- *The Power of Partnership: Students, Staff, and Faculty Revolutionizing Higher Education*, edited by Lucy Mercer-Mapstone and Sophia Abbot (2020)
- *International Journal for Students as Partners*, a scholarly journal hosted by McMaster University in Canada
- *Teaching and Learning Together in Higher Education*, a journal that features critical reflections on the processes and products of partnerships, hosted by Bryn Mawr College in the US

pointed to the social dimensions of learning and how we all learn in interactions with fellow students, friends, mentors, teachers, the educational context, and more. We're also more attentive to the emotional dimensions of learning, such as what motivates different students to persist through academic struggle, and how feelings of belonging and mattering enable learning (e.g., Lovett, Bridges, DiPietro, Ambrose, and Norman 2023). This capacious approach to learning also includes factors that can detract from learning, such as economic hardship, an ill family member, the vibration of a text message arriving on a silenced phone, and overt or subtle acts of exclusion (e.g., Verschelden 2025). And we're deeply curious about our students' learning experiences, including how different students experience a single activity since not all students (or all of us) eagerly embrace group work. Learning is far more than a cognitive activity, so many SoTL inquiries recognize and embrace this holistic experience of learning.

Institutional Environment

Some of us get involved with SoTL because we want to change our institutional environment, or at least how we experience working there. Some may want to break through the "pedagogical solitude" caused by academic cultures in which teaching is done behind the closed doors of classrooms, rarely talked about, and minimally rewarded (Shulman 1993, 6). SoTL brings teaching into the open, into conversations, and often into the broader institutional context. Katarina Mårtensson, Torgny Roxå, and Thomas Olsson (2011) demonstrate that SoTL activities, even at research-intensive universities, can increase professional interest in teaching and foster an academic culture that values teaching and learning. Joelle Fanghanel (2013) delves into what this context might look like: in contrast to traditional research cultures that are competitive and performative, she argues, campus cultures that support SoTL tend to be collaborative, democratic, "agentic," and "altruistic" (60–67).

Bruce Gillespie, Michelle Goodridge, and Shirley Hall (2024) describe how the work of three colleagues (a faculty member, a librarian, and an educational developer) followed by two similarly diverse communities of practice focused on SoTL contributed to the grassroots growth of a collegial campus culture that values teaching, learning, and SoTL. Marian McCarthy (2024) documents how more formalized pedagogical conversations and communities evolved over time at University College Cork, Ireland, showing that through SoTL practice and programming "we build up a language of theory and practice over time that invites us to problematise our teaching and our students' learning," which became "ingrained in the culture until it is a way of being, as well as a way of knowing" (112).

The Profession

Some of us engage in SoTL as part of our work as professionals, with SoTL serving as "an example of the profession building its own knowledge base for its practices" (Booth and Woollacott 2018, 545). In some countries, such as Australia and the United Kingdom, national professional standards frameworks for higher education position SoTL as one of the activities that "demonstrates to learners and other stakeholders the professionalism that colleagues and institutions bring to teaching and/or supporting learning" (AdvanceHE 2023, 2). Based on those frameworks, institutions may support and nominate academic teachers to be promoted through various levels of fellowship, making SoTL an integral component of professional development for some academics.

Even in contexts without such standards or expectations, some of us pursue SoTL because we're committed to advancing the broader knowledge about teaching and learning in higher education. Indeed, Shulman asserted that it's our responsibility as academic teachers to "contribute to the larger profession" by sharing our SoTL inquiries (1999, 15). He described this as a move toward making teaching "community property" (1993, 6), claiming that SoTL is the best way for the individual teacher and, more importantly, for the whole profession of postsecondary teaching to evolve. Ryan Martin explicitly extends this sense of duty to the profession by arguing that we also have an "obligation to share our findings with other teachers... so future students will also see the benefits" (2018, 67).

The Public Good

Finally, some of us take Boyer's original vision to heart and engage in SoTL because we want our work to make the world a better place. Based on a project that mapped the range of goals and influential contexts for existing SoTL projects, Shirley Booth and Lorenzo Woollacott (2018) analyzed a large sample of published articles from 2010 to 2016 to see how SoTL is both described and practiced. They found that the predominant goals for doing SoTL are practical and professional, similar to those we've described above. But they also identified some SoTL inquiries with aims that are moral, ethical, or societal and that emerge from cultural or political concerns. Although those goals might not be the norm, Carolin Kreber (2013) suggests that SoTL ultimately can contribute to "social justice in the world" by changing how practitioners view the purposes of higher education and their roles within it (11). Echoing this, Peter Felten and Johan Geertsema (2023) make the case for "recovering the heart of SoTL" by resisting the pressures to professionalize SoTL and recommitting to Boyer's original vision of "scholarly work on teaching and learning...[rooted in] curiosity or a desire to address the holistic needs of students and the world" (1106). Nancy Chick and Jennifer

Friberg (2022) take this one step further, calling for an explicitly "public SoTL" that challenges SoTL practitioners to "[step] up and [contribute] our expertise in conversations about the crises that face our communities, nations, and the world" (2).

SoTL has great potential to help us identify systemic barriers within and beyond higher education, and to minimize them in evidence-based ways. For example, after analyzing in-class discourse on race in four courses across two Norwegian universities, Yael Harlap and Hanne Riese (2022) highlight the frequency of "we" that conflates whiteness and nationality, "they" for racialized Others and non-Norwegians, and the colorblind denial of race altogether—practices that reflect the broader social taboos across the country. This project illuminates how the classroom can reflect and reinforce the systemic barriers beyond the university; Harlap and Riese call for research on teaching interventions that "interrupt talk that centres a white 'we' and marginalizes racialized Others, … so students emerge with more nuanced, knowledgeable, historicized and contextualized perspectives on … the world around them" (1234).

Your Why

Many more scholars around the world have contributed to this "Why SoTL?" conversation. The few mentioned above illustrate the sense many of us have about the ripple effects of doing SoTL. But this may be a daunting way to begin. You probably didn't pick up this book to make the world a better place, so let's come back to you. To echo and adapt the Boyer quote from early in this chapter, we invite you to consider that the goal of SoTL:

> is not only to prepare [academic teachers] for productive careers but also to enable them to live lives of

dignity and purpose; not only to generate new knowledge [about teaching and learning] but also to channel that knowledge to humane ends; not merely to study [teaching and learning] but to help shape [higher education institutions] that can promote the public good (Boyer 1990, 119).

Those of us who do SoTL often grow, and perhaps even thrive, because of the inquiries we do and the communities we join through the process. As we will explore throughout this book, engaging in SoTL can enhance our sense of purpose, efficacy, meaning, and connection in our work lives, as well as contribute to the larger societal mission of higher education. *That* is a powerful answer to the question "Why SoTL?" In the next chapter, we will dig more deeply into why *you* might (or already do) do SoTL.

Questions for You

We invite you to explore these questions in individual reflection or collegial conversation:

- How might you define SoTL? What is it, and what is it for?
- Do you find Boyer's vision of SoTL inspiring or daunting, or both? Why?
- Of the five reasons to do SoTL described in this chapter (from teaching to the public good), which one or two do you find most appealing and motivating right now? Why?

Supplemental Materials

- Worksheet: An Expansive View of Learning
- Matrix: Analyzing Some Definitions of SoTL

CHAPTER 2

Why You?

In chapter 1, we shared some common reasons that motivate academic teachers to participate in the Scholarship of Teaching and Learning (SoTL) and some of Boyer's (1990) arguments for doing this work. In this chapter, let's turn to you. There are many different reasons for engaging in SoTL, and these reasons can change over time. You might have a general sense that you want to try SoTL, or perhaps you have an idea you want to explore but don't know where to start. Or maybe you're an experienced SoTL practitioner looking for a chance to reorient or recharge. Whoever you are and why you're here, we invite you to consider the ideas in chapter 1 that resonated with you, and to surface the specific experiences, hopes, and curiosities that bring you to SoTL. In the pages that follow, we'll encourage you to reflect and write, so have your favorite writing tools handy.

In this and subsequent chapters, you'll find our prompts for you to reflect—on what you do, what you think, what you'd like to do and think, and why. If devoting time to such ideas feels unfamiliar or awkward to you, know that SoTL invites (or even requires) reflection. In the tenth anniversary issue of *Teaching &*

Learning Inquiry, Gary Poole and Nancy Chick (2022) share a taxonomy of seven kinds of introspection found in SoTL based on the previous eighteen issues of the journal. Mirroring this chapter's notion of SoTL's ever-widening ripples—beginning with an individual and expanding outward toward broader implications (figures 1.1 and 2.1)—reflection in SoTL often focuses specifically on ourselves (what we believe, who we are, what we do, and why) and our students (what they believe, who they are, what they do, and why). It also takes the form of thinking deeply about the contexts that inform us and our students. Our reflection is also (and often) as wide as the field of SoTL: what it is, what its strengths and weaknesses are, and what its "outer edges" are (Poole and Chick 2022, 2). And we think carefully and critically about SoTL as a community, especially "how we treat each other as peers" (Poole and Chick 2022, 2). These moments of "evaluating and theorizing SoTL" (the work itself and who's involved) are part of the field's "commitment to growing both outward by welcoming new colleagues and inward by monitoring how we act on (or don't) the values of the field" (Poole and Chick 2022, 10).

In this book, you'll find that much of the reflection we invite—some of it narrow in scope, some of it quite wide—is meant to guide you in developing your SoTL inquiry. The reflective and writing prompts, as well as the "Questions for You" at the end of each chapter, are more than simply questions for you to ponder. Instead, we recommend you pause when you come to them. Sit back, consider our prompt, and notice how you respond. Give yourself time to fully answer and follow where your thinking takes you. Write down your thinking, so you have a chronicle of your ideas as they develop; you can return to them later, and perhaps even share them when you're ready to share.

We also encourage you to reflect with others by talking with trusted colleagues about the questions and ideas in this chapter. As we (the authors) think about our own SoTL journeys, many of those moments of reflecting on what matters to us occurred in community and conversation with others—in workshops, in hallways, over coffee, in Zoom, via email. Reflection isn't limited to solitary thinking and writing and indeed is often richest when it's a shared experience.

Reflecting on What Matters to You

We invite you to reflect on what matters to you by considering how any of the "Many Reasons to Do SoTL" from chapter 1 speak to you (see figure 2.1.) We hope that, by following these ripples outward, you'll begin engaging in SoTL, start a SoTL project, or reimagine SoTL in a way that feels authentic and meaningful to you.

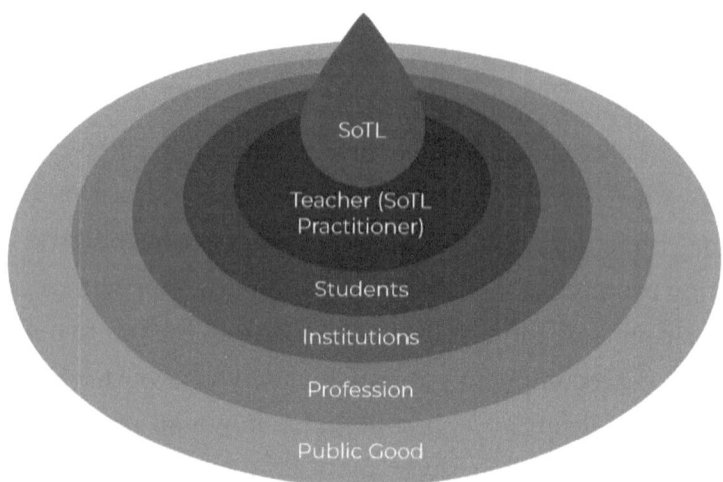

Figure 2.1. Reflecting along the ripples of reasons to do SoTL introduced in chapter 1.

You may work through all six prompts or skip to one or two that jump out to you. What's most important is that you take the time to think about what really matters to you so that your priorities guide the SoTL work you do. In chapter 3, we'll consider various entry points into SoTL— *how* and *where* to start—so for now don't worry about how SoTL works or what it looks like. Focus here on *why* you do it. Your *why* will guide your *how*.

Reflecting on Yourself

We'll start by encouraging you to reflect on yourself (i.e., your identity and your current circumstances) before thinking about the work you do. Who you are shapes what you do and what motivates you. Thinking through different aspects of your professional and personal identity can help you understand why SoTL might matter to you. Different aspects of identity evolve over time, and doing SoTL may influence your sense of self in ways that shape your career, so think about who you are right now and how you hope to develop in the future.

Your Disciplinary Self

Your disciplinary background is an important part of your identity as a scholar and academic teacher. As is the case for all of us, your discipline shapes how you think about knowledge, evidence, meaning, truth, rigor, learning, and much more. In the aptly titled chapter "Square One: What Is Research?" in *The Scholarship of Teaching and Learning In and Across the Disciplines*, Gary Poole, a psychology scholar who championed SoTL in Canada and elsewhere, reminds us that people from different disciplinary backgrounds define "research" very differently, and that these differences "touch upon the very purpose of research and the relationship between the studier and the studied" (2013, 136). Indeed, as we illustrated in chapter 1, even the term "research" may not resonate in all contexts, so an early step in venturing into SoTL should be to reflect on what "research" (or "scholarship," "inquiry," "creative activity," or whatever term you use) means to you.

Reflect

To bring you back to Poole's "square one" idea, we look to a set of prompts inspired by the research autobiography exercise developed by librarian Margy MacMillan which she shared at a SoTL symposium in 2016 (Chick 2019b, 10–11; MacMillan 2016):

- What are your early memories of doing meaningful research? What inspired your curiosity, and what made this research meaningful and memorable to you?
- In your professional work now, what is research? How do you do it? What do you do first in a research project? Then what? Then what? How do you know when it's done? What is its goal, result, or outcome?
- What five words do you associate with the kinds of research you most like doing?

As you proceed through this book, consider how a SoTL inquiry might connect to your answers to these questions.

Your Positionality

Beyond your discipline, other aspects of your professional or personal identity may inform how and why you engage with SoTL. Your positionality—or your social identities like gender, race, geographical location, socioeconomic class, ability, and more—may elevate some interests, commitments, and concerns

> **BOX 2.1**
>
> **Nancy's Disciplinary Self**
>
> My disciplinary background has always been important to my SoTL work. Coming from literary studies, "research" to me is a quiet, private, reflective, recursive activity. Literary scholars do research driven by the questions, "What does it mean?" and "How is it significant?" The "it" is typically a text or set of texts (e.g., novels, poems, scholarly analyses of the literature, theoretical pieces, contextual materials). We explore these questions by thinking deeply about what we've read, reading again, seeking and reading additional texts, thinking some more, writing, reading and thinking more, writing some more, and so on until we achieve an intuitive sense of coherence and completion. This understanding of what "research" means to me is inseparable from how I approach the SoTL projects I'm involved with: I'm interested in the texts students create—from formal essays to discussion posts to annotations of readings—and how they're meaningful.

in your work life that you want to center in how you do SoTL. For example, Peter's family history, with sharp contrasts between relatives who did and did not attend university, means he is particularly interested in the learning and well-being of students who are first in their family to pursue higher education.

Reflect

What about you? Consider the following questions to reflect on your positionality:

- How do parts of your identity motivate your teaching, research, or other professional activities?
- How does your positionality suggest possible areas of focus for your SoTL? For example, might you be particularly interested in student mental health and well-being, or the learning experiences of international students, those who are first-in-family, or women in science?

Consider how these aspects of your identity might inform and guide your SoTL inquiry.

Your Career Stage

Your career stage is another important part of your professional self. Drawing on our adaptation of Boyer at the end of chapter 1, we invite you to think of SoTL as a way to craft your own "productive career" that allows you to construct a work life "of dignity and purpose" (Boyer 1990, 119). What this looks like for you will vary over time. If you are just starting out in academia, your professional pressures and obligations will be different from a mid- or late-career academic. That's also the case if your professional appointment is contingent, such as adjunct or sessional instructors, or in a "third space," like an academic developer (Loukopoulou 2022; McIntosh and Nutt 2022).

Regardless of your career stage and trajectory, research by KerryAnn O'Meara, Aimee LaPointe Terosky, and Anna Neumann (2008) has shown that academic teachers in the US generally describe their careers as positive and purposeful when they are "carving out strategies to make meaningful contributions," for example, by "putting students first," "making long-term commitments to community engagement," "taking teaching seriously," and "making their scholarly learning … top priorities" (2008, 20–21).

BOX 2.2

Why Not to Do SoTL

Perhaps the most common reason not to do SoTL is a lack of time. This is an especially high hurdle if using your time for SoTL might conflict with larger goals like career advancement. If your institution doesn't support and reward teaching improvement or scholarly activity related to teaching, then you should think carefully about how much time and energy you can dedicate to SoTL, especially if you're on the path to a high-stakes evaluation. You might also have other commitments that demand your attention, making SoTL difficult or impossible right now. We don't want you to see SoTL as a burden or obligation. Instead, we encourage you—if you're able—to approach doing SoTL as an opportunity for sustained and collegial work that will help you feel more effective, purposeful, connected, and maybe even joyful.

Reflect

The questions below can help you explore how SoTL might fit into your career trajectory and even contribute to it feeling positive and purposeful:

- Given where you are in your career, what are your current professional responsibilities, ambitions, and opportunities, and how much professional time and attention can you give to SoTL right now?
- What do you want the next five to ten years of your career to look like? How could SoTL fit into or support that future?

- In what parts of your work do you find joy or fulfillment? How might SoTL enable you to spend more time and energy doing these activities?

Your answers to these questions can help you develop a SoTL practice that's tailored to your broader career goals.

Your Collegial Self

Finally, an important part of yourself is your connections to other people. Even if you're used to working independently—for instance, as the lone instructor in the classroom, the solitary scholar in your research, or the single author of your publications—your sense of self is influenced by others. Lee S. Shulman has said that one of the motivations and consequences of engaging in SoTL is to "put an end to pedagogical solitude" (1993, 6). Most researchers and scholars, he said, are automatically "members of active communities" rife with disciplinary conversations, idea-testing and -sharing, and critical feedback, but such generative communities devoted to teaching are rare and often have to be created. Much of Katarina's research has focused on academics' "significant conversations" about teaching in which they "make sense of experiences, where they deal with problems, and plan and evaluate actions" (Roxå and Mårtensson 2009, 556). This research has suggested that most Swedish academics have fewer than ten colleagues for such conversations (550).

You may already have trusted colleagues with whom you talk about teaching, or you might want to seek out new ones. The good news is that Roxå and Mårtensson's research suggests that these "conversation partners could be found anywhere": in your own or other disciplines, in your department or other departments, on other campuses, and even outside of higher education

(551). Indeed, in chapter 1, we started with Behari-Leak's description of her first ISSOTL conference, which she described as "one of the most engaging and meaningful professional experiences I have had in a while" because of the "generosity of and interaction with" others at the conference (2020, 5). As you'll see in chapters 11 and 12, you'll find plenty of opportunities to connect with SoTL colleagues in meaningful ways.

Reflect

These questions can help you reflect on how and why your collegial connections matter:

- With whom do you—or would you like to—talk about teaching and learning?
- When and where do—or could—those conversations occur? How could you make them happen more often, or for longer periods of time?
- What do you talk about when you talk about teaching and learning? If you find some of these conversations unconstructive (e.g., complaining about students), how might you redirect them to be more meaningful and constructive?

What you surface about your colleagues here may provide the inspiration for a SoTL inquiry, or perhaps the foundation for a collaborative one.

Reflecting on Your Teaching

As an academic teacher, you're always learning about teaching. Your subject matter evolves as new research emerges, the world changes, or your interests shift. The students in your classes change, as do their needs and motivations. Your approach to teaching matures as you gain more experience, engage with fellow teachers, and perhaps teach in different formats and contexts. And with the growth of SoTL and other kinds of pedagogical research, new knowledge about effective teaching is constantly emerging.

 Reflect

These questions can guide you in exploring aspects of your teaching:

- What are your strengths as a teacher? How do you know, and how could you build on these strengths to enhance your teaching?
- In what ways do you most want to grow and change as a teacher? What would you need to learn or understand to support this development?
- How is your teaching informed by different aspects of the context in which you teach? For example, how does class size (i.e., the number of students you teach), the modality of your teaching (e.g., in-person or online), type of institution (e.g., teaching- or research-focused), or when you're teaching (e.g., during a politically charged historical moment, just after a global pandemic) shape your teaching practice?
- What do you do to make visible and assess student learning? Given SoTL's panoramic view of learning described in chapter 1, how might you expand or enhance your assessment practices?

A SoTL inquiry can help you better understand and respond to your responses to these questions about your teaching.

Reflecting on Your Students and Their Learning

Since a key goal of SoTL is understanding and improving student learning, it makes sense to reflect on what you know about your students and their learning before you even begin. One of our greatest lessons in years of doing and supporting SoTL is that student learning is complex and that we—all of us—are often wrong about our students. Our assumptions about what they know, who they are, and how they're learning (or not) may turn out to be flawed (Poole 2018; Popovic and Green 2012). This faulty ground can lead us to make ineffective choices in how we teach our students. Stephen Brookfield's *Becoming a Critically Reflective Teacher* encourages us "to investigate where our common sense assumptions come from," especially those that "are in the air of the professional culture we've grown up in, accepted uncritically because colleagues, textbooks, and experts have told us this is how teaching works" (2017, 21–22). In this way, the "L" in SoTL also points to *our own* learning.

Reflect

Use the questions below to explore your understanding of your own students, and perhaps to push up against the limits of that understanding.

- How would you describe your current students? Who are they–including but not limited to demographic details? For instance, where do they excel, and where do they struggle? When do they seem to learn deeply? What do they value and hope for? What do they want to do with their lives? And how do they differ from one another in these aspects?
- Given your responses to the above questions, what are the implications for what motivates students and how they learn?
- Most importantly, are you sure about your responses? How do you know?

- When you talk with colleagues about students, what do you tend to talk about? How can your collegial conversations about students inform (or perhaps distort) your understanding of students?

Your responses to these questions can be the start to powerful SoTL work.

Reflecting on Your Institutional Culture

Your institution plays a significant role in your work life, not just because it's where you spend a lot of your time but also

---

BOX 2.3

Peter's Evolving Focus on Student Learning

My early SoTL inquiries centered on understanding and enhancing my students' abilities to apply a core disciplinary skill, analyzing primary sources in history. I saw many students struggle to read visual sources, and I wanted to do a better job of helping them develop this skill. To do that, I drew on my training as a historian to analyze student writing about and annotations of diverse primary sources. One of the things that those inquiries showed me is that students' beliefs and prior knowledge profoundly shape their learning. Slowly, my SoTL inquiries shifted in that direction, exploring students' attitudes towards history and confidence in the classroom. To do that work, I began to draw on my training in oral history to conduct interviews of current and former students. That approach opened my eyes to just how much students' identities and relationships influence their learning in and beyond my classes. So although student learning remains at the heart of my SoTL journey, my vision is now much broader than disciplinary skill—and my SoTL questions and methods have evolved.

because its culture—that is, its traditions, norms, and patterns of behavior—informs many of your priorities. You can understand your institution's support for SoTL activity by thinking across two dimensions (Miller-Young, Anderson, Kiceniuk, Mooney, Riddell, Hanbidge, Ward, Wideman, and Chick 2017, 3):

1. explicit information about what it values (e.g., institution type, mission, performance criteria, policies, budgets), and
2. its implicit teaching and learning microcultures (e.g., what individual teachers talk about, how they talk to each other, how some teaching practices are embedded and taken for granted, whether colleagues consult SoTL or other research on teaching and learning [Roxå and Mårtensson 2015]).

Plenty of academic teachers engage with SoTL without a SoTL-friendly institutional context, but they're aware of this disconnect and often seek supportive cultures off campus (more about this in chapter 12).

Reflect

These questions can guide you in thinking about what you might expect (or not) from your institution as you engage with SoTL:

- How does SoTL fit within your institutional culture, including its explicit values and implicit microcultures? If it doesn't fit well right now, what aspects of the institution's culture, values, or microcultures might SoTL support or be supported by?
- In what ways does your institution align with Boyer's belief that higher education's purpose is "not only to prepare students for productive careers but also to enable them to live lives of dignity and purpose; not only to generate new knowledge but also to channel that knowledge to humane

ends; not merely to study government but to help shape a citizenry that can promote the public good" (Boyer 1987, 119)?
- How confident are you in your understanding of your institutional culture's approach to SoTL? In other words, just as our beliefs about students sometimes are rooted in false assumptions or lore, the same might be the case here. How might you learn more by, for example, reading policy institutional documents or talking to experienced colleagues?

Your responses to these questions may inform your orientation toward and practice of SoTL.

Reflecting on the Profession

As we explained in chapter 1, SoTL originated with Boyer's desire to expand "what it means to be a scholar" beyond "the tired old teaching versus research debate" (Boyer 1990, xii). Building on this expansion, Shulman (2001) considered the implications of teaching and research as more than just things we do but also parts of our profession as postsecondary educators, claiming that "Each of us in higher education is a member of at least two professions: that of our discipline, ... as well as our profession as educator" (2). He argued that these two professions aren't separate, but instead they are "intersecting domains" in which "we bear the responsibilities of scholars—to discover, to connect, to apply and to teach" (2). A SoTL lens blends our professional responsibilities as scholars of a discipline and of teaching, inviting both disciplinary and more general inquiries about teaching and learning.

Reflect

These questions can guide your reflections on how SoTL can bring together what Shulman describes as your "two professions":

- What is your discipline as a whole grappling with in relation to learning and teaching? For example, STEM fields are engaging seriously with active learning and issues of equity, and many disciplines are wrestling with how generative AI is changing what and how students should learn.
- If your institution uses a framework for national or disciplinary professional standards, how might you explore one part of that framework as it applies to your specific practice?

A SoTL inquiry inspired by your responses here will bridge what may at times feel like a deep divide between different aspects of your work.

Reflecting on the Public Good

As you saw in chapter one, a foundational vision of SoTL is for it to contribute to the public good in some way. As illustrated in Booth and Woollacott's analysis of published projects (2018), SoTL inquiries can tackle moral, ethical, or societal questions or issues that directly speak to cultural or political concerns. But they don't have to be explicit about such big or abstract ideas to contribute to a better world. In fact, Randall (Randy) Bass argues that questions about "'student success' [are] the proxy for the larger problem of 'human success'" (2020, 19). He explains, "The classroom is connected to the larger world, whether it is responding to the world as it erupts and intrudes, prepping the next generation of problem-solvers to handle the most existential challenges, or seeking to realize the promise of higher education to speak to our higher values" (2020, 19).

 **Reflect**

As you reflect on these questions, think about your commitments to the public aims of SoTL:
- What motivates your professional work and your teaching? Do you have concerns about the public good (e.g., sustainability, democracy, justice) that could—and should—influence how you approach and do SoTL?
- What would it look like if your SoTL spoke to your "higher values" (Bass 2020, 19)?

Doing SoTL That Matters To You

We hope this chapter has helped you think deeply about the things that matter to you so that the SoTL you do is meaningful. As you'll learn in section 2 of this book, all elements of project development, design, and dissemination will be informed by the motivations that give you a sense of purpose, so refer back to your reflections from this chapter as you read the remainder of the book—and as you do SoTL.

These motivations will also help you think about your SoTL audience(s), or for whom you're doing SoTL. On some level, you're engaging in this work to affect your teaching and to help students learn, whether in the short- or long-term. Yet since SoTL is a form of scholarship, it's also conducted for a broader audience of peers (e.g., within your discipline, in the same geographical location, across disciplines, for educators more broadly), some of whom will offer critical review and feedback and some of whom will learn from and apply your work. An awareness of these audiences for your SoTL will inform many of the decisions you make as part of your SoTL project, such as the literature you draw on (chapter 5) and your mode of inquiry (chapter 7). In the end, there's not one "right" way to do SoTL, but how you balance these two aspects of your SoTL (speaking both to your own motivations and to a scholarly community of peers) will shape how you approach the SoTL inquiries you do.

We close by admitting that each of us (Nancy, Peter, and Katarina) has answered our own "Why SoTL?" questions differently at different stages of our careers. We persist because we've found something in SoTL that feels meaningful, a touchstone that makes this work professionally and personally fulfilling, and that changes over time. We expect that will be true for you, too, starting with taking the time to think deeply about why you're drawn to SoTL right now.

Questions for You

We invite you to explore these questions in individual reflection or collegial conversation:

- What are your "whys" for being a teacher? How has this evolved over time?
- What about your "whys" for doing SoTL? How has this evolved over time?
- What's the relationship between your "whys" as a teacher and as a SoTL practitioner?
- What role has SoTL played, if any, in the evolution of your sense of professional purpose?

Supplemental Materials

Chapter 2 Compiled Reflection Prompts

SECTION 2

Taking the Journey

CHAPTER 3

SoTL Entry Points

> "What if inside every teacher was a scholarship of teaching and learning (SoTL) project waiting to be brought to life?"
> —Gary Poole (2018)

Whether you're new to SoTL or if you're experienced and eager to try something new, you might be asking, "Where do I start?" You might have a general idea of what interests you based on your responses to [chapter 2](#)'s reflection questions, or maybe you have a big idea for an inquiry, but you don't know what comes next. Perhaps you see so many possible SoTL questions that you don't know which to choose, or you just want to give SoTL a try but don't know what area would be most worthwhile. This chapter will help you think through these kinds of questions by describing eight possible entry points for beginning a SoTL inquiry (figure 3.1):

1. Follow your curiosity
2. Reframe a problem
3. Surface prior knowledge
4. Probe a belief
5. Explore your context
6. Consider variation
7. Fill a gap
8. Honor your commitments

Think of these entry points as doorways into a big space where you'll begin your SoTL project. You might find that you have more than one overlapping entry point; they are not mutually exclusive. No single entry point is better than another, so consider easing into what may seem like new or different territory by exploring one or two that feel familiar. Alternatively, if you're feeling bold, you can explore one or two that feel less familiar—or even explore all of them to see what possibilities each opens up for you.

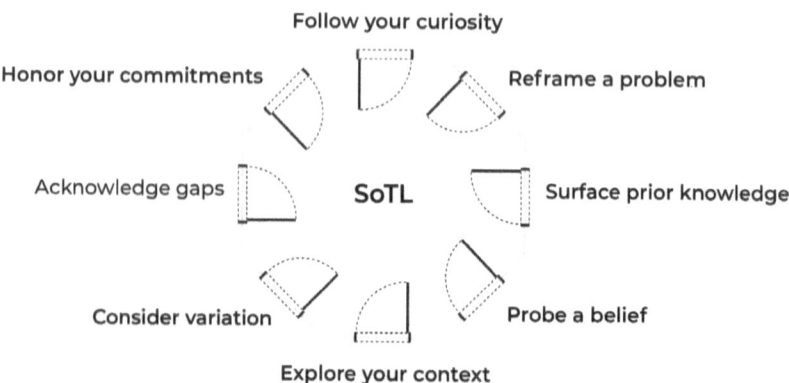

Figure 3.1. Eight possible entry points for beginning a SoTL inquiry.

The SoTL Space

In framing these as entry points, we're drawing on two foundational metaphors in SoTL, both of which present SoTL as a *space*. In the first, SoTL is a "big tent" (Huber and Hutchings 2005, 4). One of the implications of this metaphor is that there are many ways to enter SoTL, and no one is at the door checking credentials or blocking anyone's entry. As a result of this accessibility, "a wide range of work can thrive" within the big tent (Huber and Hutchings 2005, 4).

The second foundational metaphor focuses on what happens inside this tent: it's a "trading zone" where "scholars from different disciplinary cultures come to trade their wares—insights, ideas, and findings—even though the meanings and methods behind them may vary considerably among producer groups" (Huber and Morreale 2002, 73). The trading zone helps us imagine what we might do and how we might interact once we enter the big tent of SoTL, whether for the first or the twentieth time. (Perhaps unsurprisingly, this metaphor comes from scholars in anthropology and communication.) Mary Taylor Huber and Sherwyn P. Morreale explain that a trading zone contains a diversity of groups (as suggested by the title of their book, *Disciplinary Styles in the Scholarship of Teaching and Learning*) and thrives on a balance of common pursuits and understanding across differences. This balance is delicate because SoTL invites academics from many disciplines, nationalities, commitments, and other aspects of professional and personal identity that make it simultaneously rich and complex. As you saw in chapters 1 and 2, the people within this big tent bring these various identities, so like other multi- and interdisciplinary fields, this diversity makes SoTL a "low-consensus" field, one that encompasses a range of methods, literatures, and vocabularies (Biglan 1973; Donald 2002; Miller-Young and Chick 2024, 5). An underlying assumption of SoTL is that this diversity is a strength: the wider the range of approaches, inquiries, and practices, the larger the contribution to knowledge and the stronger the field becomes.

The metaphor of the trading zone captures this strength and reminds us that participants come with intentions to both give and receive. But another aspect of this diversity is that sometimes people bring expectations for the high consensus within their specific discipline, resulting in assumptions that some goods in SoTL are more valuable than others. In this way, some SoTL communities—like any other academic community—can mirror the inequities and toxicity that exist within the academy and in our world, rather than recognizing strength in diversity. We encourage you to keep in mind this metaphor of the trading zone as you pursue your inquiries, design your projects, and encounter colleagues with approaches and practices that are different from yours.

One way to keep the implications of these metaphors in mind is by reflecting on some "essential ways of knowing and doing" in SoTL spaces, or "a SoTL mindset" (figure 3.2; Chick 2023). Framing the field using spatial language aligns with our belief in *contextualizing,* or acknowledging that our work is inherently located in a specific place and time. As we explain above, the trading zone metaphor also captures the foundational moves of *multidisciplinary thinking* and *collegiality*. Both of these moves require a sense of humility, including the *pedagogical humility* of acknowledging that there is so much we don't know about our students' learning and the connections between teaching and learning more broadly (recall "Reflecting on Your Teaching"

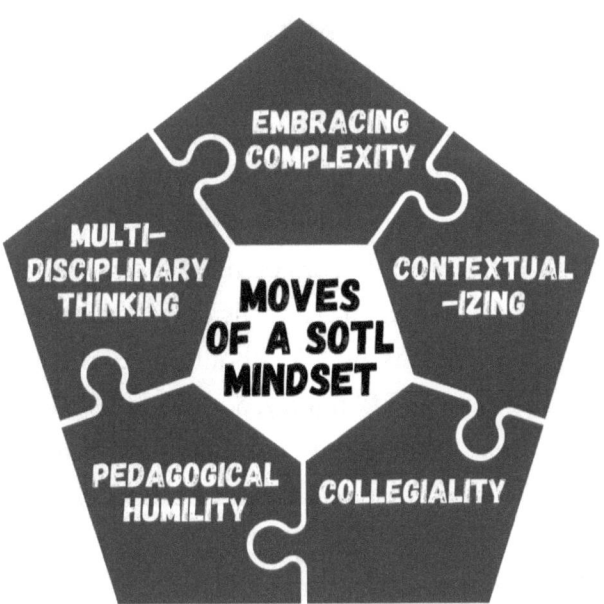

Figure 3.2. Five key moves of a SoTL mindset. Adapted from Chick (2023).

and "Reflecting on Your Students and Their Learning" in chapter 2). They also call us to *embrace complexity* in teaching and learning. You'll find that these moves are threaded throughout this book, both explicitly and implicitly. To learn more, see the supplemental materials on the book site.

We wrote *The SoTL Guide*, not just this chapter, with these metaphors, moves, and their implications in mind. There is no *one way* to begin, develop, conduct, or share a SoTL inquiry, and there's room for great diversity in SoTL spaces. We hope the chapters in this book make these processes inviting and accessible, regardless of where you come from and where you want to go. This chapter focuses on a first step: where to start? How will you step into the big tent, and what will you do in the trading zone? (See the SoTL Entry Points worksheet resource.) Below, we elaborate on eight possible entry points.

Entry Point 1: Follow Your Curiosity

Academics are curious people. The same curiosity that drives your disciplinary work can be an entry point for your SoTL inquiries. The spark that lights this fire in SoTL can come from many different places. It may emerge from a classroom experience or a conversation with colleagues, or you might encounter something new at a conference or in an academic development program. If you notice yourself thinking a lot about one of these moments, perhaps it's ripe for a SoTL inquiry. Some SoTL colleagues keep "curiosity journals" where they compile their ideas, questions, and flashes of insight that might later become the foundation for an inquiry.

Another common source for inquiry occurs when something you're reading piques your curiosity. This might come out of your routine reading practices, a recommendation by a colleague, or a selection in a reading group. Or you might decide to read some SoTL literature, perhaps after consulting with a SoTL colleague or a librarian who can guide your search. See box 3.1 for how Nancy's habit of reading sparked a curiosity that led to a SoTL inquiry.

 Reflect

Use the prompts below to spark your curiosity:
- What are you curious about as you think about your students, their learning, or their experiences as learners?
- What puzzles you when you teach a specific course, concept, or skill?
- What new ideas about teaching and learning have you encountered that have stuck with you?

BOX 3.1

Nancy's Reading Practice: An inspiration for SoTL Inquiry

I read a lot, a habit developed in my background in literary studies. I'm often inspired by what I read, so this practice is a common entry point for my SoTL work. A recent example began when I wondered how my colleagues at my private residential campus in Florida (in the US) would handle teaching about race after the state government passed legislation banning teaching about diversity, equity, and inclusion in all public education. I'd read Tanja Burkhard's "Facing Post-Truth Conspiracies in the Classroom: A Black Feminist Autoethnography of Teaching for Liberation After the Summer of Racial Reckoning" (2022) and was so moved by Burkhard's experience as a self-described "Black German immigrant woman" confronting the limits of typical ground rules for controversial class discussions that I reached out to the author in appreciation (2020, 34).

Later, in wrestling with the political context for teaching on campus, I revisited the article and integrated parts of it into a few workshops on navigating the new (and not new) complexities of teaching about race. A little later, a workshop participant (Lucy Littler, a colleague in the English Department at my institution) emailed me to report that the different approach to these fraught discussions—inspired by Burkhard—was especially helpful. I then invited Lucy and Tanja to develop a collaborative SoTL project inspired by the lessons of the original article. As of February 2025, we've collected artifacts from two of Lucy's classes and will be collecting them from Tanja's classes this semester. This project, and these new relationships, began with simply reading an article.

Entry Point 2: Reframe a Problem

A second SoTL entry point is grounded in Randy Bass's early and influential article on SoTL, "The Scholarship of Teaching: What's the Problem?" (1999). He encourages us to approach "problems" in our teaching and in our students' learning with an orientation to inquiry, rather than a source for shame or reason for solitude. In our disciplinary research, he notes, we often *want* to talk with colleagues about the interesting and vexing problems we encounter, but we may not do the same with our teaching. Framing teaching and learning "problems" like research problems puts them "at the heart of the investigative process" (1999, 1). He illustrates with his own example of overhearing his nineteenth-century literature students assume they were reading certain texts because he thought they were good, when in fact he assigned them for their "insight into a particular way of seeing in the nineteenth century" (1999, 6). This moment of accidental eavesdropping surfaced for Bass a significant problem he'd missed for years: he'd never "taken into account—nor endeavored to discover" his students' assumptions about what and why they were reading in his literature classes. This discovery led to the inquiry at the heart of his article.

In a more recent article, Bass revisits this notion of a teaching "problem" to acknowledge that many of the problems at the center of a SoTL inquiry don't have a single easy solution. In fact, he argues that "we need to think of the problem of learning—and by implication, the problem of higher education—as a complex, *wicked* problem,… a social or cultural problem that is difficult or impossible to solve" (2020, 6). These problems call for greater effort to understand their complexities, efforts that may lead to messy and multiple answers and give rise to more and new questions (see chapter 4 for more on this). Bass isn't alone in emphasizing the "wicked problems" in teaching and learning. A longitudinal, collaborative, global project systematically mapped out the Grand Challenges of SoTL, or five such problems that call for greater SoTL inquiry, including: how to develop critical and creative thinkers, how to encourage students to be engaged in learning, and how identities affect both teaching and learning (Scharff, Capocchiano, Chick, Eady, Friberg, Gregory, Loy, and Maurer 2023).

Below are some comments we've heard over the years, which serve as examples of the kinds of classroom problems that invite inquiry:

- "Every semester, students struggle most with the concept of ___."
- "I want to figure out how best to support first-generation students in my class."
- "Students frequently tell me that my feedback isn't clear."
- "In small-group activities, some students tend to dominate while others remain silent."
- "No matter how I teach, students repeat the same error patterns over and over."
- "Some of my students have such high test anxiety that their performance on exams doesn't seem to reflect their actual learning."
- "My students do well on the regular reading quizzes, but they're not drawing connections between the readings in their final papers."

Again, rather than seeing these observations as complaints, deficits in your students, or embarrassing failures in teaching, Bass (1999) encourages us to revisit them as "an invitation … to ongoing investigation" (1).

 **Reflect**

Use the prompts below to follow Bass's example of reframing a problem to open lines of inquiry for you:
- What is a problem with your students' learning experiences that's plagued you, puzzled you, piqued your interest, and/or pleased you? How is it a problem? When does it happen? How does it become visible to you, and what does it look like? What are its consequences?
- What is a problem, complexity, or phenomenon about students' learning in your discipline that you and your colleagues keep returning to? How can that be explained or understood more deeply?

Entry Point 3: Surface Prior Knowledge

If we dig beneath some of the problems we encounter in teaching and learning, we'll often find something cognitive psychologists have been telling us about for years: students don't come into our classes as blank slates. See, for example, *How People Learn II: Learners, Contexts, and Cultures*, a consensus report commissioned by the US National Academies of Sciences, Engineering, and Medicine to "[review] and synthesiz[e] research that has emerged across the various disciplines that focus on the study of learning from birth through adulthood in both formal and informal settings" (National Academies 2018, 2). One of the key findings in the report is that:

> Prior knowledge can reduce the attentional demands associated with engaging in well-learned activities, and it can facilitate new learning. However, prior knowledge can also lead to bias by causing people to not attend to new information and to rely on existing

schema to solve new problems. These biases can be overcome but only through conscious effort. (2018, 4)

What students bring with them has tremendous implications on their learning, which is both good news and bad news. Some of the problems you envisioned above may be the result of students' prior knowledge and beliefs. The classic video "[A Private Universe](#)" (1987) vividly illustrates how erroneous preconceptions can lead even highly accomplished students astray. Similarly, students' beliefs about learning, intelligence, and their own identities—all formed well before they take your course—can powerfully shape how they respond to difficulty, confusion, and disappointment in educational settings, so drawing out their beliefs is especially important (Corwin, Ramsey, Vance, Woolner, Maiden, Gustafson, and Harsh 2022).

But students' prior knowledge can also be an asset (Moore 2023). When students bring "robust and accurate" knowledge and beliefs that are appropriately activated, they're poised to learn deeply (Lovett, Bridges, DiPietro, Ambrose, and Norman 2023, 4). Indeed, differences in performance among students in your course might emerge primarily from differences in the knowledge or beliefs they came with, even if all students are learning during the course (Brod 2021). For instance, students of color, and by extension students with various kinds of minoritized identities, may draw from what Tara J. Yosso describes as six kinds of "cultural wealth" they bring to their learning, including resiliency, flexibility in language and communication skills, a strong belief in community, experience navigating difficult contexts, and motivation to challenge injustice (2005, 7).

As you think about your students' prior knowledge, then, look not only for errors and mistakes but also insights and strengths that you can mobilize to support students and their learning.

Careful attention to their preexisting knowledge and beliefs—and when and how they productively or unproductively activate them (Kapur 2016)—could be a promising entry point to your SoTL inquiry.

 Reflect

See below for some questions to help you surface what your students know (or don't know) and believe:

- What do you know about your students' prior knowledge and beliefs about your course content?
- What do you know about your students' beliefs about learning, your discipline, or themselves as learners?
- What strategies can you use to activate their prior knowledge? What strategies can they use? And how can you use that information to support learning in your course?
- Based on what students bring to your course, do you see patterns of struggle or success that might suggest lines of SoTL inquiry?

Entry Point 4: Probe a Belief

Your own beliefs also have implications for your students' learning. A classic study demonstrated that primary school teachers' expectations about their students' academic abilities significantly shape those students' learning (Rosenthal and Jacobson 1968). More recent research not only confirms this finding but also finds that secondary and higher education teachers' expectations about their students' academic capabilities influence those students' choices about what fields to study (Lee, Min, and Mamerow 2015), and that academic teachers' beliefs about students' intelligence also contribute to whether and how teachers use active learning pedagogies in their teaching (Aragón, Eddy, and Graham 2018). Clearly, what we believe about our students matters.

Gary Poole (2018) has critically analyzed the origins of our beliefs about teaching, learning, and students. He argues that too often these beliefs emerge from gut feelings, conversations with colleagues, and anecdotes and observations that we unreflectively promote to truth. This trust in our own experiences and perspectives can be helpful as part of developing what's often called "the wisdom of practice" (Shulman 2004; Weimer 2001), but Poole cautions us to be skeptical too. Indeed, research has shown that academic teachers' beliefs about students often are inaccurate (Cox 2011; Popovic and Green 2012).

Reflect

Rather than automatically trust or distrust our beliefs about teaching and learning, Poole invites us to start SoTL projects with questions about what we believe. Below are some prompts to spark this kind of inquiry:

- How would you finish these sentences?

    Today's students are ____.
    Today's students prefer ____.
    I've noticed my students are/do ____.
    My students learn by _____.

- Why do you believe each of these statements to be true?
- What does each of these beliefs lead you to do in your teaching?
- How might a different belief lead you to act (and teach) differently?

Entry Point 5: Explore Your Context

A fundamental assumption in SoTL is that you don't teach generic students a generic topic in a generic institution and at a generic moment in time. Instead, your SoTL inquiries unfold in a distinct setting, within specific conditions, and with particular participants, including you. This is why throughout this book we encourage you to embrace what Behari-Leak calls "situational ethos," or an awareness of context in your SoTL (2022, 33). In fact, this critical attention to where and when you are doing your inquiry might be your entry point.

Whether we're aware or not (and we're often not), geographical and cultural contexts inform every SoTL inquiry. In their 2013 article, Singapore-based Chng Huang Hoon and Peter Looker call for explicit recognition of this fact and illustrate their claims with Jin Li's (2009) observation about fundamental differences in students' culturally-informed goals for learning: "the most significant purpose of learning for the Chinese students is the need 'to perfect oneself morally,'" in contrast to the American purpose of "the development of mind and understanding" (2013, 140). This difference suggests that a SoTL inquiry in one cultural context might pursue questions or be influenced by frameworks that are different from a similar inquiry in another context. Similarly, Chaka Chaka, Thembeka Shange, Sibusiso Ndlangamandla, and Dumisile Mkhize, scholars in South Africa, assert that SoTL in Africa should "take full consideration of the historical, sociocultural, and economic realities of the students and faculty, while being sensitive to global realities," rather than "simply focusing on the cognitive dimension of teaching and learning at the expense of the harsh historical and socioeconomic realities of students and faculty" (2022, 7, 18). Location matters in SoTL, even though

Chng and Looker wisely caution against oversimplifying "where" in our inquiries.

Time is another potentially salient aspect of context. For example, the disruptions of the COVID-19 pandemic produced a flood of inquiry on the experiences of students and academics, including two special issues of the journal *SoTL in the South* on "Lessons for the Future of SoTL in the Global South" (2022, 2022a). And in the US, Laura Cruz and Eileen Grodziak even suggested that the pandemic might have prompted whole new categories of SoTL questions, including "What's your story?" (2021). And, of course, time and timing can matter even without a global crisis. Think about those experiences in your teaching when a practice or activity that's seemed to work well in past classes no longer engages students in the same way. These instances can be frustrating while teaching in the moment, but they might also become an entry point into a SoTL inquiry.

Reflect

Below are some questions to guide you in thinking about your context as a way to start a SoTL inquiry:
- What aspects of your context are distinctive or seem particularly significant to you? How might you use those as entry points in your SoTL inquiry?
- Is something changing in your context that might be worth examining more closely?
- Are there SoTL inquiries that you find inspiring or challenging that you'd like to adapt to your context?

BOX 3.2

Katarina's SoTL Context: An Inspiration for Engaging in SoTL

I work as an academic (faculty) developer in a research-intensive, centuries old, Scandinavian university. One of my main tasks is to support academic teachers and leaders to develop teaching and learning in this context. In the early 2000's there was an initiative in this university to award excellent teaching, and the development of the criteria for the award was inspired by Carolin Kreber's "Teaching Excellence, Teaching Expertise, and the Scholarship of Teaching" (2002). The concept of SoTL turned out to resonate well with academic teachers in a research-intensive environment. However, as described in chapter 1, there was—and still is—an ongoing effort to translate the meaning and idea of SoTL into the Swedish language. Also, because many academics are researchers in their disciplines, in this context SoTL is not described as research but more as an inquiry-based, academic approach to teaching and learning. My colleagues and I were inspired to introduce the concept of SoTL in the professional development activities for academic staff, and to construct support with SoTL as a foundation. In the mid 2000's the Swedish government made such professional development mandatory across Swedish higher education, and part of the commonly agreed upon goals for such higher education teacher training (comprising ten weeks in total) was a SoTL-approach (Lindberg-Sand and Sonesson 2008). So, since then, I have conducted SoTL inquiries largely focused on how to support others in Sweden in becoming engaged in SoTL and also how higher education institutions can benefit from embedding SoTL in their institutional culture.

Entry Point 6: Consider Variation

Delving more deeply into Gary Poole's invitation to approach your beliefs and assumptions with skepticism, you might productively scrutinize your idea of "my students," "our students," and even "students." Although it can be tempting to fret about "kids these days," research consistently shows students learn at varied paces and demonstrate their learning across a wide spectrum of performance. Indeed, large-scale research in the US has demonstrated that student learning, engagement, and experiences differ more *within* a single institution than they do *between* institutions (Blaich, Wise, and Crawfordsville 2011, 8; Kuh 2003). Similarly, as we shared above, Yosso's research points to distinct assets students of color bring to their learning experiences (2005).

What happens when we take an inquiry approach to student variation in our courses, programs, and institutions? What might you learn, for example, if you identified certain types of student performance (e.g., students who consistently score well on your exams, or students who struggle on an early assessment but then perform better later in the course) and then partnered with those students on a SoTL inquiry to document their study practices? These students' study behaviors—or perhaps their mindsets—might offer clues for how you can help more students do well in the course. Or perhaps you want to better understand how different aspects of students' identities (e.g., year of study, gender, ethnicity) might influence their experience in your course. Hannah Jardine, Gavin Frome, and Elizabeth Griffith (2023) deliberately recruited a diverse group of student partners to join an inquiry and course redesign project focused on a chemistry lab at the University of Maryland College Park (US). They then co-designed the partnership work with students to include both individual and shared work, creating multiple opportunities for individual student voices to contribute to curricular and pedagogical reform, recognizing the variety of students' experiences within this large course.

Students also bring different backgrounds and identities into our courses. Research in many contexts shows significant and enduring correlations between student learning or persistence in higher education and certain demographic characteristics, such as family income, race or ethnicity, gender, and whether the student comes from a family with higher education experience. SoTL inquiry could dig into one or more of these characteristics in a particular course or related to a specific learning goal. For example, Annika Fjelkner-Pihl (2022) used social network analysis to consider how the study behaviors and academic performance of students at a Swedish university are influenced by their immigration status, gender, and length of daily commute to campus. Katelyn M. Cooper and Sara E. Brownell (2016) used interviews to explore the specific experiences of LGBTQIA+ students in an active learning science course at a university in the US. And Alison Cook-Sather and Morgan Cook-Sather (2023) offer a "mother/daughter, faculty/student" case study of one US student's experiences with university exams as a legally blind undergraduate (1).

Reflect

The granularity and nuance of these SoTL studies reminds us how important it is to understand the distinctiveness and diversity of students' experiences.

Use the questions below to consider the differences among your students:

- What groups of students (or even profiles of students) would you like to—or need to—learn more about as learners in your course?
- How might different students experience your courses (or specific activities in your courses) differently?
- What might you learn by inquiring into the study habits of students who tend to be successful in your course, or students who initially struggle and then succeed?

Entry Point 7: Fill a Gap

Scholarly inquiry often begins by noticing gaps in existing literature or research. What hasn't been studied, said, or imagined—a missing perspective, a neglected topic, a new way of understanding an old idea—often becomes the starting point for new inquiries. Many articles even point explicitly to the need for further research. Each of these types of gaps call for inquiry.

As a field, SoTL is relatively young, and there is still so much to learn about postsecondary teaching and learning, especially within different contexts. There are plenty of underexplored topics, perspectives, contexts, and methodologies in need of SoTL inquiry. Projects that step into the gaps created by existing perspectives and practices contribute a great deal to what we're collectively learning as part of a larger profession of educators. For example, the journal *SoTL in the South* publishes SoTL focused on and/or written by authors in the global South, a context that's not often found in the SoTL journals that (perhaps inadvertently) focus on the global North. SoTL projects that challenge dominant perspectives can yield powerful results that identify the cracks in that dominance, as in Athulya Aby's (2022) exploration of the role of colonialism in Indian architectural education. Plus, Shanthni

Selvarajan, Sue Chang-Koh, and Lavanya Balachandran's inquiry into residential college education in Singapore (2022) reminds us that projects that study well-researched topics in new or different contexts contribute to a more complex and fuller understanding of teaching and learning.

Other prominent gaps relate to the focus and approaches of most published SoTL. For instance, in a project emerging from one of SoTL's large international collaborations, Karen Manarin, Christine Adams, Richard Fendler, Heidi Marsh, Ethan Pohl, Suzanne Porath, and Alison Thomas (2021) (Australia, Canada, and the US) systematically analyzed the contemporary SoTL literature, discovering that "By far the most common focus in our sample was on [an] instructional tool or approach" (359). In other words, published SoTL tends to focus on "what works" for teaching and teachers (Hutchings 2000, 4) more than on student learning and students. Using Booth and Woollacott's (2018) taxonomy based on published SoTL (see chapter 1), these projects would fall in a large domain they call "the didactic," or practical projects that aim to change teaching practice (540). In their conclusion, Booth and Woollacott call attention to the relative dearth of projects that engage with values, power, and expectations ("the moral/ethical domain"), or with the "societal" domain's attention to "the demands and needs of society and how higher education is addressing those needs" (2018, 542–543).

In another international collaboration across Australia, Canada, UK, and the US, Aysha Divan, Lynn O. Ludwig, Kelly E. Matthews, Phillip M. Motley, and Ana M. Tomljenovic-Berube (2017) analyzed 223 projects published in three SoTL journals finding a balance of qualitative, quantitative, and mixed methods studies, but no instances of humanistic methodologies like close reading. Their finding echoes a widespread call for more SoTL studies using humanistic or artistic methods (Bass and Linkon 2008; Bloch-Schulman, Wharton Conkling, Linkon, Manarin, and Perkins 2016; Chick 2013; Hovland 2021; Manarin 2018; Potter and Wuetherick 2015). Similarly, in analyzing the narrative structure of SoTL publications, Faye Halpern (2023) points out the dominance of what she calls "the story of redemption" because any and all struggle is resolved, so she outlines a handful of alternative and "radical" structures that are possible but rarely embraced in SoTL (1, 11). Similarly, Nancy Chick, Laura Cruz, Jennifer C. Friberg, and Hillary H. Steiner (2023) explore the relative absence of projects and publications about failure in SoTL. And stylistically, Helen Sword (2019) calls for more first-person voices to humanize the telling of SoTL stories after documenting the prevalence of third-person perspectives and pronouns in published SoTL.

Reflect

These trends mean that significant and promising gaps exist in SoTL scholarship—and in day-to-day SoTL work—that might feel like invitations for you. The prompts below may help you identify some gaps:

- Are you aware of any gaps in what's currently known about teaching and learning—perhaps as described by something you've read or what you've noticed from a preliminary literature review? What interests you about this gap?
- Which gaps noted in this section (if any) speak to you, and how might you start to fill them?
- What underexplored perspectives, contexts, identities, and cultures do you or your students bring to teaching and learning that you could explore in a SoTL inquiry?

- Even if your SoTL inquiry follows a well-trodden path, what is different about your or your students' context or experiences that would offer new insights on a familiar topic?

Entry Point 8: Honor Your Commitments

A final entry point, which might actually be your primary one, emerges from your professional and personal commitments: the values, identities, perspectives, and desires for change that motivate your work, and perhaps also your life. SoTL can be an opportunity and a vehicle for bringing these commitments more deeply and systematically into your professional work.

Whether we notice or not, education and SoTL are deeply rooted in cultural, political, economic, and historic contexts. To illustrate, Canadian SoTL scholars Kelly Hewson and Lee Easton (2022) reflect on the grave violence done by education and educators to Indigenous people in Canada and then draw on queer and decolonial theories to call for SoTL scholars to directly confront both the harms and the possibility of a different vision of education. On a more individual level, Craig Nelson, in "Student Diversity Requires Different Approaches to College Teaching, Even in Math and Science," (1996) identifies himself as a scientist who once assumed that the STEM fields exist outside of "particular cultural constraints," so there was no need to worry about teaching "in a culturally biased way" (165). As his article title suggests, though, he learned over time that "much of what I took as neutral teaching practice actually functions to keep our courses less accessible to students from non-traditional backgrounds" (165). In this confession, Nelson declares what became a commitment that guided his subsequent SoTL work focused on exposing and countering these inequities in the classroom.

Crystena Parker-Shandal, a Canadian scholar, illustrates this entry point in her 2023 study of undergraduate student participation rates in classroom discussions. Parker-Shandal's inquiry emerged out of her concern that students with marginalized identities "such as first-generation university students, students with accessibility needs, and female, Black, Indigenous, and students of colour" (1) would not feel welcomed to engage in class discussions, which would restrict both their own learning and the depth of class discourse. Committed to rectifying this inequity, she surveyed more than 600 students in one academic program about their experiences in and perspectives on discussions. Her findings demonstrate that students have complex and nuanced views: "Most students indicated that they wanted to participate and be engaged" (14) and believed that "moments of contention developed their sense of empathy and understanding" (13). Yet many at times would "self-silence to protect themselves from the emotional and psychological toll of sharing" (14). Parker-Shandal concludes with recommendations for instructors to learn how to facilitate difficult conversations with diverse students in their classrooms so that "students learn to practise tolerance and inclusion and to become participatory citizens" (15).

This commitment elevates Boyer's claim that higher education's purpose is:

> not only to prepare students for productive careers but also to enable them to live lives of dignity and purpose; not only to generate new knowledge but also to channel that knowledge to humane ends; not merely to study government but to help shape a citizenry that can promote the public good. (1987, 119)

His call for institutions of higher education, as well as their individual teachers and SoTL scholars, "to meet today's urgent academic and social mandates" (1990, 13) underscores the importance of critically analyzing the ideologies and systems that are the foundation for education and for SoTL. They highlight the interconnectedness of education and what some call "the real world." They also illustrate the need for more SoTL scholars to amplify their commitments in their work.

Reflect

This isn't to say that your commitments need to mirror those described above. Consider what's important to you and how these issues might be guiding principles in your work. Revisit your responses to the prompts in chapter 2, and see if any of those rise to the level of a commitment. You may also use the prompts below to help you surface any commitments that could guide your SoTL work:

- What do you think the purpose of higher education is? Is it serving this purpose right now? How do (or might) your classes contribute to this purpose?
- What's are you committed to as an educator and a person? What do you care about, deeply? How do (or might) you bring those values into your teaching, and how do (or might) your students experience these commitments?
- What commitments do you see in your students? How do (or might) you facilitate learning experiences that speak to these commitments?

Beyond Entry Points

Our goal with this chapter framed around a variety of entry points for starting a SoTL project is to be inclusive and inviting.

If it feels instead like choice overload, or being so overwhelmed by options that you can't actually make a choice, revisit your responses to the prompts in chapter 2. We want to encourage you to do SoTL that matters to you, so we hope at least one of the eight entry points above resonates with one or some of your responses to your reflections in chapter 2.

It's also worth noting here that, even though we've spent a lot of time setting you up for a thoughtful beginning, where you start isn't necessarily where you'll end. Plenty of SoTL journeys take a turn when something new or interesting emerges along the way, so don't worry or get stuck trying to select *the perfect* starting point. Often what is most important is just to take that first step.

BOX 3.3

Katarina's Professional Commitment

As an academic developer at my research-intensive university, my main task is to support the development of teaching and learning across all disciplines and educational programs, as well as to provide professional development opportunities for all teaching staff and educational leaders in this university. A main challenge—and ambition—is to provide both individual and collegial support. The key features of SoTL, inquiring into teaching and learning *and* sharing findings with others even if mainly locally, therefore provide a useful strategy and core value underpinning academic development activities in this context. I focus both my professional practice and my research activity in this area of SoTL and professional/organizational development.

Questions for You

We invite you to explore these questions in individual reflection or collegial conversation:

- What strengths and assets do you bring to the "trading zone" in SoTL? How can you make these visible to others in the "big tent"? And what are you seeking from others who are in this "trading zone"?
- Which entry point(s) seem most appealing to you right now? Why?
- Do any of the entry points challenge you to think about SoTL inquiry differently? Why?
- If you have a SoTL inquiry in mind, what happens if you try approaching it from different entry points?

Supplemental Materials

- Worksheet: SoTL Entry Points
- Chapter 3 Compiled Reflection Prompts

CHAPTER 4

Meaningful SoTL Questions

"Every scholarly and professional field is defined by the questions it asks." —Pat Hutchings (2000)

Meaningful inquiry begins by asking meaningful questions. Although we understand what makes something significant in our disciplinary work, that judgment may be less clear in the context of SoTL. We also know that disciplinary research needs to have implications for others in our field. The same is true for SoTL, but how do we make something as individualized—and even idiosyncratic—as what happens in our classrooms meaningful to someone else? Who are the other people who'll find our inquiry meaningful? What questions may be relevant to both ourselves and others?

What Is "Meaningful"?

In "Learning Matters: Asking Meaningful Questions", Anthony (Tony) Ciccone (2018), former director of Carnegie Academy for the Scholarship of Teaching and Learning (CASTL), offers some guidance on how to ask questions that are meaningful to ourselves and others. (See box 4.1 on the origin of this guidance.) He identifies five characteristics of SoTL questions that "matter":

1. they "arise from a troubling, surprising, or perplexing teaching and learning experience that seems to defy a simple solution" (16),
2. they are "truly consequential to us as teachers and to our students as learners" (17),
3. they compel us "to gather new and different information about our students' learning or at least look differently at what we've been getting and thus to teach and assess differently" (17),
4. they "raise more questions than [they] answer and thus invite further research" (19), and
5. they have "the potential to go beyond the problem from whence [they] arose to elucidate some key insights into big issues about student learning and the frameworks that would explain them" (20).

Ciccone's list underscores how "particularities" often drive meaning (Shulman 2014). Determinations of what's *troubling, surprising, perplexing, consequential,* or *new and different* are situated within a particular perspective (the teacher's), local context (the specific learning environment, the content taught, the student group), and moment in time (now). You saw in the previous chapters that SoTL inquiries are often—and ideally—grounded in what's meaningful to the practitioner, and entry point 5 (chapter 3) illustrated the influence of a specific context on teaching, learning, and SoTL. When COVID-19 prompted higher education to suddenly switch to remote instruction, questions about students' well-being, home environments, and digital access became more meaningful for many academic teachers and institutions (Cruz and Grodziak 2021).

Ciccone also stresses that effective SoTL questions don't lead to easy answers, quick fixes, or closure, a reminder that some SoTL problems are "wicked." This may be unsettling for some. Indeed, recall Halpern's (2023) critique of published SoTL that too often tells a story of "linear progress and endless self-improvement" (13). While simple explanations can be tempting, SoTL tends to embrace complexity because students and student learning are complex (see chapter 2). SoTL is most meaningful when it dives into the difficult and messy nature of learning.

BOX 4.1

Nancy's Orientation to SoTL Questions

Much of this chapter is inspired by Tony Ciccone's suggestion that the most important step in developing a SoTL project is its question. In fact, I learned how to do SoTL in the statewide program he facilitated across twenty-six campuses in the US, and the beginning of the program brought the participants together for five days. One of those days was devoted *entirely* to workshopping everyone's question. This experience is why I later invited him to write his chapter, "Learning Matters: Asking Meaningful Questions" in my edited book on "critical moments of practice" (Ciccone 2018).

And, of course, our experiences with teaching are complex, too. If teaching and learning were simple, we could answer our SoTL questions by asking a colleague or just following our intuition in the classroom. Even when we start a SoTL journey with what might seem like a simple question, the inquiry process typically leads us into more challenging terrain (see box 4.2 for Peter's experience with such terrain).

Ciccone's description of meaningful SoTL questions as "truly consequential" resonates deeply with us. SoTL's attention to holistic conceptions of learning and the entire learning experience strikes us as highly consequential. For example, one Canadian and three South African scholars—Elizabeth S. Ndofirepi, Raazia Moosa, Maureen J. Reed, and Mandivavarira Maodzwa-Taruvinga—developed a novel inquiry comparing nearly 850 students at two urban universities in their two countries (2023). Because the

---

BOX 4.2

Peter's Evolving Questions

When I wanted to understand why my advanced history undergraduates struggled to analyze visual but not textual sources, I ended up exploring not only what students do when they encounter primary sources (my original question) but also the ways that their prior knowledge and beliefs shape their approaches to meaning-making in history (Felten 2005). As Ciccone suggested, I didn't find an easy fix to the problem of students struggling to make sense of visuals. However, by better understanding the complexities of students' learning, I have been able to develop new classroom exercises designed to help students recognize their assumptions about images before they begin to engage with them as primary sources.

learning experiences and outcomes of first-generation students are profoundly shaped by the academic and personal roles they must juggle as students (e.g., family care responsibilities or the need to work), these scholars designed their inquiry to explore questions about:

> (1) the multiple types of roles that are experienced by first-generation students relative to their peers; (2) the relationship between the perceived ability to balance multiple roles and academic outcomes (academic self-efficacy, university adjustment, and grades) in first-generation and non-first-generation students and; (3) the relationship between the perceived ability to balance multiple roles and psychosocial variables (academic resourcefulness and resilience) in first-generation and non-first-generation students. (Ndofirepi, Moosa, Reed, and Maodzwa-Taruvinga 2023, 24)

As illustrated in this example of inquiry into the impact of culture in Canada and South Africa on the educational experiences of these students, SoTL questions are consequential when they inquire into the intersections between teaching and learning and the significant challenges facing communities and the world—or what Boyer called the "public good" (1987, 119). Richard Gale (2009) frames these important "questions of value" as those that "speak to and influence issues of significance to society, addressing our values writ large, what we need to understand as members of a local, national, global community" (7). Carolin Kreber (2013) calls on us to do SoTL "as if the world matters" because "questions around what our students learn, who they become, and how they choose to engage with the world once they graduate from university matter fundamentally to the well-being of our local communities and wider society" (13, 68).

Recall, for example, Parker-Shandal's (2023) study of class participation by students with marginalized identities (in chapter 3), to name just one. The significance here comes from the nature of the questions you ask, not from the size of the project or the number of participants.

A Taxonomy of SoTL Questions

Pat Hutchings, a leader at the US's Carnegie Foundation who played a pivotal role in SoTL's early evolution, together with Mary Huber and Lee Shulman, developed a taxonomy of SoTL questions that's frequently used to frame SoTL projects by identifying the instructor's "'opening lines' of inquiry" where a study starts to take shape (2000, 1; see also Hutchings describing the taxonomy). She identifies four types of SoTL questions, specifically those that ask about "what works" or "what is," those that begin with "visions of the possible," and those that generate "a new conceptual framework for shaping thought about practice" (2000, 4–5; see table 4.1).

The first two types of questions in this taxonomy are usefully simple as a heuristic for SoTL's inclusion of efforts to both *improve* and *understand* learning and teaching.

- *What works?* questions lead to comparative studies aimed at implementing an intervention, testing a potentially better strategy, and trying to fix a problem. For instance, earlier in this chapter we described how Ndofirepi, Moosa, Reed, and Maodzwa-Taruvinga (2023) ask questions about "what works" to support first-generation students in different university contexts.
- *What is?* questions lead to nuanced descriptions designed to reveal something about learning and teaching, in all of their complexities. Recall from chapter 3 the Cooper and

Table 4.1. Taxonomy of SoTL questions (Hutchings 2000, 4–5)

Question Type	Description	Question Stem
"what works"	"seeking evidence about the relative effectiveness of different approaches"	*What works?*
"what is"	"describing what it [a particular approach or intervention] looks like, what its constituent features might be"	*What is?*
"visions of the possible"	wondering what if? in trying something that's new (or new to you)	*What if?*
"formulating a new conceptual framework for shaping thought about practice"	leading to a new way of understanding something, or "theory building"	*What does this ultimately help us understand?*

Brownell (2016) article that asks "what is" the experience of LGBTQIA+ students in an active learning biology class. The third and fourth types are less simple but no less valuable.

- *What if?* questions inspire projects that start with a sense of play or experimentation in trying something to see what happens, with no expectations of what those consequences might be. In terms of how these projects are ultimately designed (more about this step in chapter 7), they tend to be structured as comparisons of before and after the "something" (similar to *What works?*) or narrative descriptions of what happens (similar to *What is?*). For example, Mariolina Salvatori (2000) began a SoTL inquiry by asking what if students could make visible their struggles with complex literary texts; to explore this question, she developed a "difficulty paper" that prompted students to describe and analyze their struggles (more on this in chapter 7).

- Projects that lead to "new conceptual frameworks" rarely begin with that intention. They may begin with one of the other question types but, sometimes accidentally, produce a new way of making sense of something. Dianne Fallon's (2006) seemingly simple inquiry about what is "reveal[ed] about students connect class content to the world around them" in a single assignment led to surprising results, so her puzzlement inspired her to create a developmental "taxonomy of diversity learning outcomes, behaviors, and attitudes" based on how her white students in a majority-white state in the US responded to talking about race in class (411, 414).

In our experiences doing and supporting SoTL projects, hearing about them at conferences and other events, and reading about them in published form (Booth and Woollacott 2018; Manarin, Adams, Fendler, Marsh, Pohl, Porath, and Thomas 2021), the majority of SoTL projects follow questions about *What works?* and *What is?*.

Based on these experiences, we offer a nudge. Despite an eagerness to try out something that might improve student learning, *What is?* questions that seek understanding are often the best place to start a SoTL project. In fact, recalling Poole's (2018) observation that we often base our assumptions about our students on faulty or incomplete information, perhaps one of the most important questions we can ask in SoTL is, "What is *really* happening here?" (Chick 2024). If we try to improve or fix or intervene based on incorrect assumptions, we may change nothing—or even make matters worse.

A helpful illustration comes from Annika Fjelkner Pihl's (2022) study of students in a business program that attracts students from non-academic backgrounds, as well as many who commute for about one hour to get to campus. Fjelkner Pihl, an experienced teacher at a teaching-intensive institution in Sweden, observed that students clustered together in various groups in the classroom:

> I see them form pairs and groups. I see them struggle, and subconsciously seem to know which of the students will do well, seemingly without an effort on my part, which of them will have to struggle but will get there in the end, and which of them will probably do everything backwards or not at all and will try to argue their way to a pass grade anyway." (Fjelkner Pihl 2022, Prologue)

A year later, she met the same students, but fewer now, and noticed that "about half the group sit with fellow students they seem to know very well, grouped together in the front half of the lecture hall. Scattered around the outskirts of that group are other students, who sit alone or in pairs, but seemingly demonstratively outside the larger group" (Fjelkner Pihl 2022, Prologue). Based on this observation, she embarked on exploring (and eventually wrote a dissertation on this topic) the student-student relations by asking *What is really happening here?:* how do these students form their own personal networks and how do these student networks influence their academic achievements? She then used what she learned from this project to develop a model for supporting students to develop more diverse study networks to support their academic achievements. Like many *What is?* SoTL inquiries, her question evolved over time as she learned more; as Fjelkner Pihl's example illustrates, sometimes a seemly simple question can unfold into a long-term and consequential inquiry.

That's not to say you should avoid *What works?* questions. Many of us do SoTL because we want to get better at teaching, and we want our students to learn more deeply and enduringly. In fact, one of SoTL's goals is to improve teaching and learning in a certain context (see chapter 1; Larsson, Mårtensson, Price, and Roxå 2020). Knowing *what works* matters. However, these questions can be challenging to answer in a satisfying way. You might, for instance, teach so few students that comparisons are difficult, or maybe you don't feel comfortable setting up a rigorous comparison that gives only some of your students a specific benefit (e.g., regular active learning exercises, study groups, metacognitive activities) but not others (Bunnell, Felten, and Matthews 2022). Our point is simply that you should critically reflect on just how well you know *what is* before you jump into trying to figure out *what works*.

Extending Hutchings's Taxonomy: SoTL Questions in Context

Hutchings's taxonomy is a helpful place to start with framing your SoTL question, but there are a few ways to get more specific that we encourage—that is, by also asking, *Where?*, *When?*, and *For whom?* (see figure 4.1). These additions carry forward our emphasis on the importance of context by changing the nature of the questions you ask, and your particular context may call for very particular questions. Chng Huang Hoon, Katarina Mårtensson, and Brenda Leibowitz suggest that—since SoTL always occurs in "geographical, social, cultural, and political" and temporal contexts—every *What is?* or *What works?* question should include the modifiers *Where?* and *When?* (Chng, Mårtensson, and Leibowitz 2020, 25). By comparing their experiences of supporting and leading SoTL initiatives in Singapore, Sweden, and South Africa, they demonstrate how each context produces different challenges related to commonly assumed perspectives on teaching and learning, language translations, and political issues.

An additional aspect of context, perhaps implied by *Where?* and *When?* but worth making explicit, is *For whom?* Like the other modifiers to Hutchings's questions, this one reminds us that

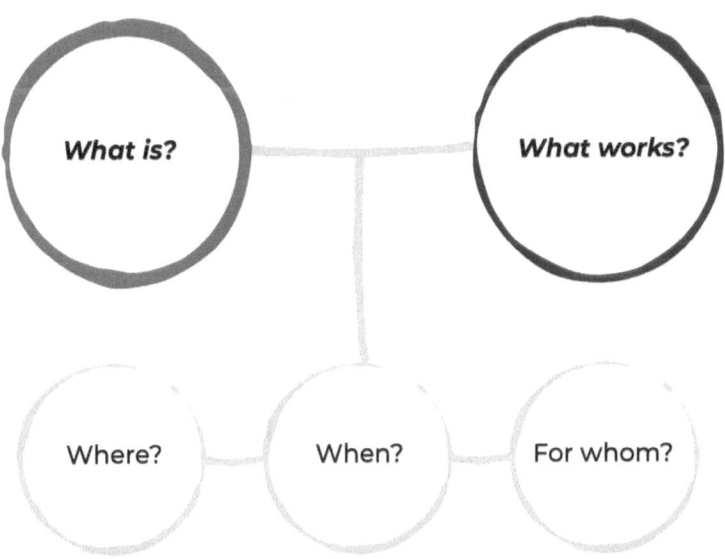

Figure 4.1. Extending Hutchings's taxonomy to include contextual questions *Where?*, *When?*, and *For whom?* Conceptualization by the authors, building on Hutchings (2000) and Chng, Mårtensson, and Leibowitz (2020).

experiences and identities vary—and matter—in teaching, learning, and inquiry. Plenty of research suggests that even students in the same program and class experience teaching and learning differently. For example, although the efficacy of active learning pedagogies in STEM courses is well documented, questions persist about whether those benefits hold for all students. Cooper and Brownell's (2016) interviews with seven students who identify as LGBTQIA+ at their university in the US in the early-to-mid-2010s surfaced many specific ways in which these students struggle—and struggle differently—with active learning in class, not the least of which includes fears about how their classmates will respond to them in these more interactive class experiences. Similarly, in interviews with twenty-five students with common "neurodevelopmental disorders" (e.g., ADHD and dyslexia) at their university in the US, Mariel A. Pfeifer, Julio J. Cordero, and Julie Dangremond Stanton (2022) found significant variation in experiences with active learning. Both inquiries grounded in asking *what works for whom?* helpfully identifies barriers to these specific students' learning, leading to recommendations for how to minimize barriers for LGBTQIA+ and neurodivergent students.

And, of course, these extended questions don't have to be just about the students in a course. Who conducts the inquiry—their identities, their specific location, at which moment in time—matter as well. In an international, collaborative, autoethnographic SoTL project, Nattalia Godbold, Dawne Irving-Bell, Jill McSweeney-Flaherty, Patrice Torcivia, Lauren Schlesselman, and Heather Smith (2021), from six institutions in Australia, Canada, UK, and the US, inquired into how aspects of their personal and professional identities influenced their experiences of SoTL. After comparing their different personal narratives, they conclude that their reflections:

> cannot be separated from our contexts and our positionality. As a group we differ in ages, career trajectories, disciplinary background, institutions, current positions, citizenship, and parenting responsibilities. We are all self-identified white women. We also acknowledge that our stories are constrained and limited by our experiences. (Godbold, Irving-Bell, McSweeney-Flaherty, Torcivia, Schlesselman, and Smith 2021, 385)

Their project reminds us that we ask questions and conduct inquiries informed by who, where, and when we are.

In figures 4.2 and 4.3, we illustrate Hutchings's taxonomy and the *Where?*, *When?*, and *For whom?* extensions with some sample SoTL questions.

So What? Asking Questions That Are Meaningful to You and Your Students

This exploration of what makes SoTL questions meaningful might have complicated your thinking about SoTL inquiry. Given the situatedness of teaching and learning and SoTL's expansive view of learning, we want to complicate SoTL inquiries enough to help you capture this reality by "representing complexity well" (Poole 2013, 141). Our hope is that this guidance also empowers you to focus on what is "truly consequential to [you] as teachers and to [your] students as learners" (Ciccone 2018, 17).

We also believe SoTL can and should be more attentive to how power shapes our teaching and our inquiries. Carolin Kreber (2013a) reminds us that the meaningfulness of SoTL questions

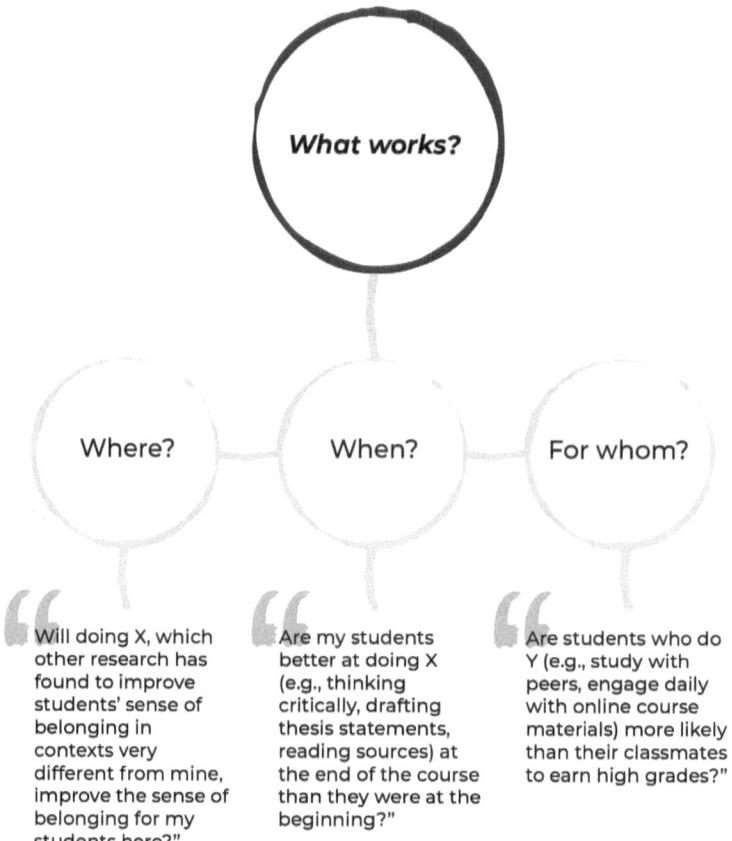

Figure 4.2. Sample *What works?* SoTL questions framed using Hutchings's taxonomy and contextual extensions.

should be examined with a critical eye to *Why?* and *Why not?* and *Who decides?* (862). In other words, who gets to decide if a SoTL question is meaningful—and who doesn't? Canadian scholars Janice Miller-Young and Michelle Yeo (2015) extend Kreber's analysis by documenting that "Questions of power and privilege in the classroom largely go unasked, so far, in the SoTL landscape" (45). We hope that our work and your inquiries will help to reorient SoTL.

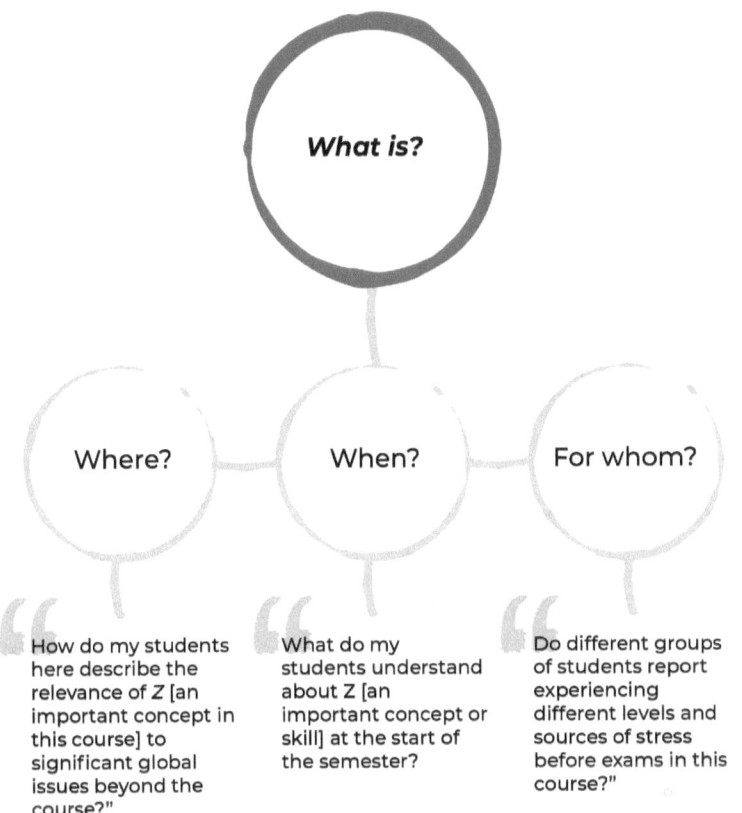

Figure 4.3. Sample *What is?* SoTL questions framed using Hutchings's taxonomy and contextual extensions.

Finally, as you think about your SoTL questions, we encourage you to continue to ground yourself in your earlier reflections about why you do SoTL (chapter 2) and where you're starting (chapter 3). We also invite you to reflect on what's possible for you to achieve in SoTL in any given moment and in your particular context. As you'll see in subsequent chapters, bigger is not necessarily better in SoTL inquiries. Inquiring into seemingly small issues, small moments in time, or even small numbers of students can be consequential if the question is meaningful.

Questions for You

We invite you to explore these questions in individual reflection or collegial conversation:

- What SoTL questions come to mind after reading this chapter?
- What kinds of SoTL questions do you tend to ask?
- What do you notice if you play with your questions by reframing them (e.g., from *What Works?* to *What is?*) or by adding modifiers (e.g., *when*)?

Supplemental Materials

- Worksheet: **Nuanced *What Works?***
- Worksheet: **Nuanced *What Is?***
- Video: Pat Hutchings talks about the taxonomy of SoTL questions in this video (3:48) produced by the Center for Engaged Learning at Elon University

CHAPTER 5

Situating Your Work in SoTL Conversations

"Imagine that you enter a parlor. You come late. When you arrive, others have long preceded you, and they are engaged in a heated discussion.... You listen for a while, until you decide that you have caught the tenor of the argument; then you put in your oar. Someone answers; you answer him; another comes to your defense; another aligns himself against you.... The hour grows late, you must depart. And you do depart, with the discussion still vigorously in progress." —Kenneth Burke (1941)

American literary theorist Kenneth Burke's (1941) description of the parlor is frequently invoked as a metaphor to frame exploring existing scholarship as an act of entering an interactive, lively, and ongoing conversation among scholars (10–111; see figure 5.1). This metaphor is foregrounded in Gerald Graff and Cathy Birkenstein's (2021) writing textbook *They Say/I Say,* which asserts that the most important "moves that matter in academic writing" are "expressing your ideas ('I say') ... as a *response to some other person or group* ('they say')" (3). This simple but foundational move of building on relevant research may feel familiar in our disciplinary scholarship, where some call it a "literature review" (or "lit review" for short) and others call it simply "research." But this essential step often suffers from "benign neglect" in the scholarship of teaching and learning (MacMillan 2018, 23; see also Healey, Matthews, and Cook-Sather, 2020).

There are good reasons for this neglect. It's easy to feel daunted by the task of finding relevant and helpful SoTL literature. In fact, we've written this chapter with more stepwise instructions and examples than some others because this part of doing SoTL can

Figure 5.1. Burke's metaphor of the ongoing parlor conversation. Adapted from Burke (1941).

feel so intimidating. Most of us come to SoTL unaware of what's in the literature, what broader topics are connected to our lines of inquiry, or even where to start looking for relevant sources. As of the writing of this book, there's no single database that brings together all relevant publications, and there aren't yet agreed-upon keywords or search terms in SoTL. Also, common higher education terms like "assessment" mean different things in different countries. Because these characteristics are more about the field than the person doing the inquiry, all of us who engage with SoTL (regardless of experience) have to navigate these challenges. The good news is that they aren't insurmountable. This is also a great place to point out that librarians make excellent collaborators in SoTL inquiries; and two librarians, Lindsay McNiff and Lauren Hays, have created a useful [online guide](#) to understanding and searching SoTL literature.

UK scholars Mick Healey and Ruth L. Healey (2023) recommend seeing this part of the SoTL inquiry process as a rigorous yet creative process, an act of "meaning-making [that] is nuanced and contextualised" and that reflects your scholarly "identities and values" (4). As we suggest in [chapter 2](#), who you are and what matters to you will, and should, guide you throughout your SoTL inquiry. Healey and Healey also stress that you can start with what you already know. If something you read or heard sparked your inquiry (see entry point 1 in [chapter 3](#)), or if you already know something about your topic, Healey and Healey recommend this prior knowledge may act as a lens for your new inquiry and a starting point for your lit review as you seek to expand on what's already at least somewhat familiar to you.

Margy MacMillan (2018), a librarian and SoTL scholar in Canada, helpfully describes the SoTL lit review as both "a process and a product" (23). In other words, looking back to Burke's metaphor, the *process* is walking into the room, listening carefully to the conversation, and then focusing on a few of the speakers who seem the most compelling, given your interests. This is the work of searching through library databases, Google Scholar, stacks of books, reference lists in interesting and relevant articles, and other sources like recorded talks, blogs, or podcasts. Later comes the *product* of the literature review, or your "oar," in Burke's metaphor. This is the visible form that appears when you share your work with others in a presentation, poster, article, or some other way. This product is your opportunity to make sense of the conversations that are relevant to your SoTL inquiry and to use that synthesis to frame and situate your own work—and ultimately to contribute your own ideas and voice to the conversation (see more about this in [chapter 10](#)).

In this chapter, we'll describe components of a SoTL lit review, including both the process and the product. We use the term "lit review" as shorthand for a range of ways you might engage with and join the SoTL conversation to ensure that your SoTL is grounded in the literature and adds something to the ongoing scholarly discourse on learning and teaching.

Process: Exploring the SoTL Literature

To help you start exploring the literature, let's go back to Burke's metaphor of the conversation in the parlor. An overarching question for your SoTL lit review will be *What do you want to contribute to existing conversations?* Before you reflect on that question, though, you'll need to figure out which conversations you want to contribute to. Be patient here because, at this early stage, you won't yet have full answers to either of these questions. In fact, holding them open as you familiarize yourself with the relevant literature can lead to a stronger lit review than a laser-focused search for a few recent publications that directly address your specific topic. With this outcome in mind, we encourage you to begin broadly.

Step 1: Listen Widely

Extending Burke's metaphor of a conversation in one parlor, we recommend starting your lit review process by visiting multiple parlors, wandering from one to the next (see figure 5.2). You might search several databases, scan the references of an article or book that has influenced you, consult with a librarian, attend a SoTL conference or a talk, or ask a colleague in your institution's teaching and learning center. This exploratory approach will give you a general understanding of what's out there, allowing you to mentally map the issues that intersect with your inquiry in some way—some closer to your topic, some farther away, but all potentially relevant and meaningful. You'll probably discover that your inquiry is connected to a larger issue that you hadn't anticipated, giving your work greater significance by tapping into some important concepts well beyond your specific topic. This kind of mapping will help you identify where you fit in the conversation(s) and what you can contribute.

We also recommend exploring parlors that are filled with voices you might not otherwise hear. A study on who gets cited in SoTL and why encourages all of us to resist focusing on those with established reputations or familiar names by instead "read[ing] widely and curiously" and reflecting on "which ideas and perspectives we reach for, and where we reach" (Chick, Abbot, Mercer-Mapstone, Ostrowdun, and Grensavitch 2021, 17). Our choices in reading and citing matter because, as the

Figure 5.2. An extension of Burke's parlor conversation metaphor to multiple, overlapping conversations. Conceptualization of Burke 1941.

authors explain, "citation signifies who's read, who's published, who's funded, who's tenured, who's employed, and who's heard" (2). In addition to being conscientious about the power embedded in citation practices, a more expansive and inclusive approach to your lit review will ensure that your Burkean parlor doesn't become an "echo chamber" (8). More broadly, you'll also contribute to the health and growth of the field of SoTL.

It's worth pointing out here that you're not writing a dissertation, so your lit review doesn't need to be comprehensive. Keep returning to Burke's metaphor, and notice that he says you're listening for "the tenor of the argument" (1941, 110). Your goal with this step is to get familiar with relevant conversations by listening widely. Give yourself the permission, time, and flexibility to follow some trails, hop up to scan the horizon periodically, and trust that paths leading to dead ends may also offer helpful lessons along the way.

An Extended Illustration

To illustrate, imagine you're developing a SoTL project to help you understand how students learn a challenging but central concept in one of your courses. One way to start would be to investigate if there are any publications about how students learn (or how teachers teach) that specific concept in your discipline. Be sure to visit that parlor to see if there's a conversation already underway. But don't stop there. To listen widely, you might also notice that your inquiry is connected to larger issues in how learning happens (figure 5.3). Your steps might look something like this:

- You might dip into the conversations about *what students do with what they (think they) already know about a topic*, which is described in some of the research as "prior knowledge" or "preconceptions." Or perhaps you explore *how students' thinking about the concept is different from ours*, sometimes written as "novice" and "expert" thinking. This may lead you to Biggs 20009, Biggs and Tang 2011, Lovett, Bridges, DiPietro, Ambrose, and Norman 2023, and National Academies 2018.
- Either of these paths might lead you to wonder about *learning as an ongoing process*, sometimes described as "developmental," or about *how much learning happens where we can't see it*, what's sometimes described as "invisible thinking" that needs to be

"made visible." At this point, you may come across Bass and Eynon 2009; Bloch-Schulman 2016; Yeo, Miller-Young, and Manarin 2023.

These explorations might then lead to some methodological possibilities for your inquiry on understanding how your students learn this course concept.

You might come across existing studies that look into how students think about a course concept by, for instance, using concept maps (Kandiko, Hay, and Weller 2013; Van Zele, Lenaerts, and Wieme 2004) or think-alouds (Bloch-Schuman 2016; Mason 2021) or annotations on a course text (Chick, Hassel, and Haynie 2009; Razon, Turner, Johnson, Arsal, and Tenenbaum 2012). Meanderings like these will take you to rich areas of research that could inform your inquiry, and that could also situate your work in conversations that already engage many educators, regardless of discipline or context. The challenge at

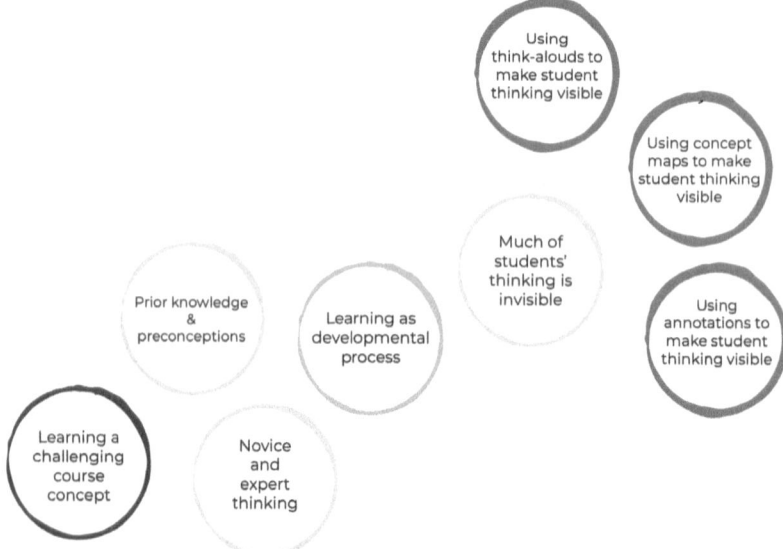

Figure 5.3. Sample steps of listening widely in the scholarship of teaching and learning (SoTL).

this point will be to decide which conversation (or conversations) you most want to join. Which conversation(s) offer(s) the most promise to help you understand your questions and eventually contribute in meaningful ways?

Step 2: Listen Deeply

After exploring several parlors, you can then focus on being strategic and systematic. You might ask yourself:
1. What are the one or two foundational texts that address the topic of my inquiry?
2. What are some recent studies that are highly relevant to the topic of my inquiry?

This deeper dive into the topic at the heart of your inquiry will familiarize you with both the origins of a key conversation (first question) and the current state of the literature (second question).

An Extended Illustration

To return to the example inquiry above, let's say that your question is grounded in a biology course and that step 1 (listen widely) has helped you focus on a specific point within your challenging course concept, namely that students bring some misconceptions to the course that make learning this concept difficult. Below is how you might listen deeply in your literature search.

MacMillan (2018) recommends Google Scholar for SoTL literature reviews. Its reach, which is far beyond any of the discipline-focused databases, aligns with the breadth of SoTL's multidisciplinarity. You can search for your topic along with a contextual keyword, such as "higher education" or "postsecondary." As of late 2023, a sample search for "student misconceptions biology higher education" brings up over 125,000 results, clearly too many. One way to start filtering such an enormous result is to look at the "Cited by" numbers. Figure 5.4 below shows an article that's over twenty years old but also has a relatively high number of citations, suggesting it might provide a foundation for your inquiry into this topic.

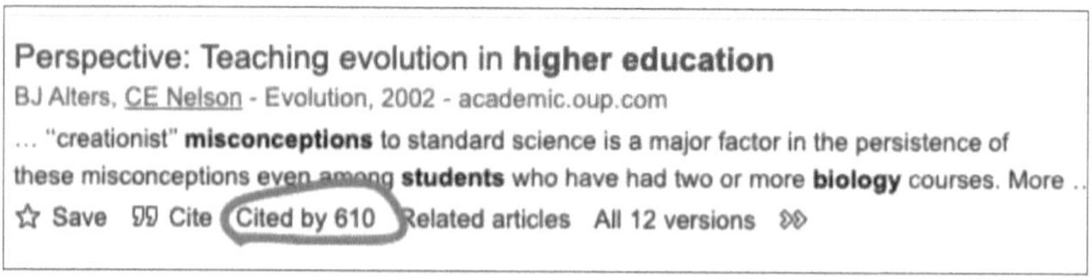

> **Perspective: Teaching evolution in higher education**
> BJ Alters, CE Nelson - Evolution, 2002 - academic.oup.com
> ... "creationist" **misconceptions** to standard science is a major factor in the persistence of these misconceptions even among **students** who have had two or more **biology** courses. More ..
> ☆ Save 99 Cite Cited by 610 Related articles All 12 versions ⋙

Figure 5.4. The "Cited by" feature in Google Scholar, used to identify highly cited foundational articles relevant to your inquiry. Screenshot by the authors.

To sort through the overwhelming output, you also could click "Since 2019" on the left to find newer sources, such as this Turkish study in figure 5.5.

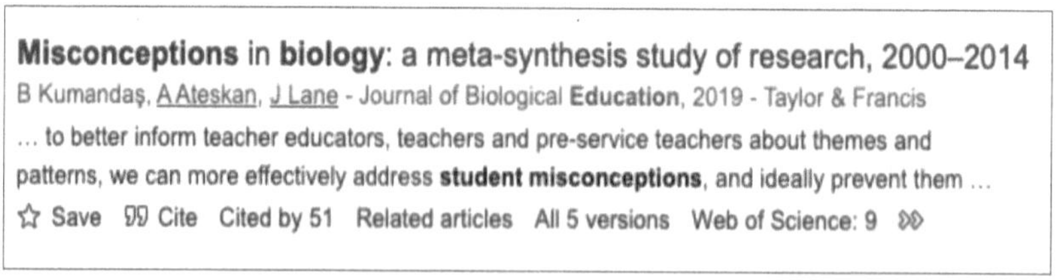

> **Misconceptions** in **biology**: a meta-synthesis study of research, 2000–2014
> B Kumandaş, A Ateskan, J Lane - Journal of Biological **Education**, 2019 - Taylor & Francis
> ... to better inform teacher educators, teachers and pre-service teachers about themes and patterns, we can more effectively address **student misconceptions**, and ideally prevent them ...
> ☆ Save 99 Cite Cited by 51 Related articles All 5 versions Web of Science: 9 ⋙

Figure 5.5. An article found by filtering Google Scholar results "Since 2019." This helps surface more recent publications. Screenshot by the authors.

You may want to situate your inquiry within the misconceptions held specifically by students in Australia, so you could add "Australia" to the search bar and perhaps remove the focus on more recent publications. figure 5.6 below shows one of the top results, a study from a biology course at a university in Adelaide.

> [HTML] Evolution: improving the understanding of undergraduate **biology students** with an active pedagogical approach
> S Buckberry, K Burke da Silva - ... : education ..., 2012 - evolution-outreach.biomedcentral ...
> ... **Students** in a large introductory **biology** course at Flinders **University**, South **Australia**, were quizzed on **misconceptions** ... of these focus on **students** in **higher education**. Bishop and ...
> ☆ Save 99 Cite Cited by 22 Related articles All 11 versions ≫

Figure 5.6. A top result from narrowing a Google Scholar search by location ("Australia"), showing a study of student misconceptions in a biology course. Screenshot by the authors.

From there, you could click the "Cited by" link to see the subsequent articles that have cited this study, and the "Related articles" link for others. And of course if any of these sources end up being especially relevant or helpful, see if their bibliography includes some foundational sources or adjacent studies you hadn't yet found. You are now listening deeply to a specific parlor conversation, and you're well on your way in your SoTL lit review.

Step 3: Identify Your Contribution

After listening both widely and deeply, you can now situate your inquiry by asking, *What do I want to contribute to these existing conversations?* In your disciplinary work, you may be used to having to find something completely original: a question, idea, or area that no other researcher has touched. This high bar is especially present in well-established disciplines with long histories of researchers generating knowledge, leaving gaps that are smaller and smaller, even as new questions arise. This would be a prohibitively high bar in SoTL, since none of us are familiar with the entire body of literature. Fortunately, the expectation for originality is different and less daunting in SoTL. Postsecondary teaching and learning are such complex, dynamic, understudied, and contextualized phenomena that they invite ongoing, widespread, diverse, and even repeated inquiries. It may be helpful to think of a puzzle with pieces of many types, sizes, and colors—but without the box cover showing us the final picture that we are trying to assemble. SoTL requires many hands to begin to put together a clear picture. And, as we've learned in recent years, that picture changes, so even more hands are needed to keep up with this puzzle.

There are several ways to think about how you might contribute to the ongoing conversation. Consider how your inquiry *complements* what's already out there. The context in which your inquiry takes place, for example, may differ in important ways from the contexts in prior studies. You may teach at an institution with fewer than 2,000 students, while the existing studies were conducted at institutions with ten times that many, or at similar institutions but in another country or with a different student population. These distinctions in context matter because the experiences of teaching and learning in each are meaningfully different. In "The Value of Contextualized Work and Aggregated SoTL Data," Lee Shulman (2014) imagines the potential of similar inquiries explored "in multiple particular settings," allowing educators to gain a fuller understanding of a topic and to make decisions based on the contextual factors that are most relevant to their own. If your lit review leads you to studies with questions, methods, or other aspects of project design that resonate with your inquiry, consider repeating or adapting them within your own context, situating your findings in relation to the original study, and calling attention to how your work complements the existing ones. In short, don't shy away from similarity: your contribution may be in differences that at first glance seem small but are, in fact, rich sites of originality.

You can also make a meaningful contribution to existing conversations simply because of your perspective. The lens you apply to your inquiry may differ from other scholars who've explored the same topic, context, or question. Perhaps, for instance, you teach courses in philosophy, and the relevant studies you've found in your lit review are based on chemistry classes. Your disciplinary lens and other aspects of your perspective may lead you to offer a question, method, or analysis new to the conversation. Whether you notice it or not, your perspective is foundational to your SoTL because "underlying any inquiry about teaching and learning are particular stances and world views about such things as how learning works, as well as assumptions about methodology" (Miller-Young and Yeo 2015, 38). As Torgny Roxå, Thomas Olsson and Katarina Mårtensson (2008) from Sweden explain, when we're explicit about the conceptual frameworks, world views, or theories we rely on, we share "models or perspectives that can be used to enrich perception, scaffold analysis and plan future practice" (281).

An Extended Illustration

In table 5.1, we've outlined how two articles on the same topic (inquiry-based learning) illustrate how some of these differences complement each other and become equal contributions. Imagine that you're doing a SoTL inquiry on inquiry-based learning and you come across these two articles in your lit review.

We could go further and unpack additional similarities and differences in the two articles, but we hope table 5.1 provides enough information to help you see that there is still plenty of room to contribute, even when you find several inquiries exploring similar questions. Recall that Shulman (2014) encouraged

Table 5.1. The complementarity of different projects about the same topic and question type. Comparing two articles.

"Integrating Inquiry-Based Learning into the Academic Literacy Course to Enhance Student Learning" by Nomakhaya Fidelia Mashiyi (2018)	"Using a Self-Determination Theory Approach to Understand Student Perceptions of Inquiry-Based Learning" by Fangfang Zhao, Gillian Roehrig, Lorelei Patrick, Chantal Levesque-Bristol, and Sehoya Cotner (2021)
First, the two studies asked What is? questions about how students experience inquiry-based learning:	
"How do undergraduate teacher-trainees experience an AL [academic literacy] course which integrates guided inquiry-based learning of its content?" (40)	"1) How do students perceive the level of inquiry in laboratory activities? 2) How do students' perceptions of inquiry differ, if at all, from the level of inquiry envisioned by the instructor?" (3)
However, they were conducted in different contexts:	
This inquiry focused on 46 second-year undergraduates in a once-a-week, 27-week stand-alone module on academic reading and writing in an education program at an unnamed university in	This inquiry focused on 114 non-STEM students in an introductory biology course that lasted a full semester (i.e., approximately 14 weeks) at an unnamed university in the US.

South Africa. Notably, Mashiyi explains that the study was also conducted against a backdrop of nationwide student protests about the increases in student fees.	
Both also used surveys with a mix of closed- and open-ended questions:	
Mashiyi's survey asked students about "their classroom experience, how the course was delivered and how it did/did not enhance their learning" (40). She explains that she intended to distribute the survey at the end of the module (late 2016), but the student protests disrupted these plans, so she had to survey the students later (in early 2017).	Zhao, Roehrig, Patrick, Levesque-Bristol, and Cotner's survey first asked students to rate "the amount of inquiry perceived in each lab" on a 0–100 scale (7), and then to describe why "the lab that best reflects inquiry" was "a good example of inquiry" and why "the lab that least reflects inquiry … does not involve much, if any, inquiry" (5). This survey was distributed after the course had ended.
The two studies were guided by different conceptual frameworks, but both used these frameworks to deductively analyze the students' responses to the open-ended survey questions:	

Mashiyi writes about using Lev Vygotsky's ideas about scaffolding, the Zone of Proximal Development, and collaboration (all part of his Sociocultural Theory for how learning happens) to code student responses. She also inductively developed her own codes when she came across responses that didn't map onto Vygotsky's three ideas.	These authors drew on psychology's Self-Determination Theory, which that claims, "three basic psychological needs must be satisfied for an individual to thrive: autonomy, competence, and relatedness" (3), to code the survey responses according to whether students felt that inquiry-based learning met each of these three needs.

similar studies conducted "in multiple particular settings" to, in the case of these studies, give us a better understanding of inquiry-based learning. Because of the differences in location, geopolitical context, discipline, perspective, and more, these two studies complement each other, amplifying each project's SoTL-generated knowledge about inquiry-based learning. Specifically, they provide overlapping findings about how students perceive inquiry-based learning, including where students struggled, what they enjoyed or valued, what they think was helpful (or not), and where they didn't recognize it at all.

If you stepped into this conversation about inquiry-based learning and brought your own context, perspective, and students' responses and thought about your own context, perspective, and students' responses alongside these previous studies, your contribution would be clear and significant. Also, the above inquiries (and the ones in the next section) rely on surveys of students' experiences and perceptions of their learning in inquiry-based learning, an important topic since this pedagogy has an explicit focus on what the students do rather than what the teacher does (Biggs and Tang 2011). If you, then, complemented these project designs by instead looking directly at student work produced in an inquiry-based learning environment, your project would be distinct and complementary in yet another important way. (See chapter 7 for more about project design and chapter 8 for more about the artifacts, evidence, or data you collect.)

Ultimately, as we've mentioned earlier in this book (and will continue to do), we have so much to learn that there are many ways you can design your inquiry to contribute to existing conversations.

Product: Connecting Your Inquiry to the SoTL Literature

Chapter 10 will focus on how to share your work when you're ready, but now is a good time to say a few things about what MacMillan (2018) calls the *product* of your lit review *process*, or how you represent it when you present or publish your inquiry. Rather than passing mentions or an obligatory list of citations of existing scholarship, she encourages you to envision this product as "a reliable guide to the conversations that… inform conducting and interpreting a study" (2018, 28–29). Through Burke's parlor metaphor, you've imagined your lit review process as listening to and joining some conversations, so now you can succinctly frame it that way for your audience. This approach elevates the written (or spoken) lit review as "a meaningful result of the study in and of itself" (MacMillan 2018, 23). In other words, just as you'll collect and analyze artifacts, evidence, or data related to student learning to help you respond to your SoTL question (see chapter 8 and chapter 9), think of "the literature as data," so the existing scholarship you've collected and analyzed also helps you respond to your question (MacMillan 2018, 23). This can be a paradigm-shifting way of thinking about the lit review. Indeed, in our experience as SoTL journal editors, we've found that reviewers (and later, readers) sometimes focus on a lit review as the most interesting or useful part of an article.

A 2020 study by Canadians Alicia Cappello and Janice Miller-Young, a graduate student in library studies and a SoTL scholar who partnered on a SoTL citation analysis, offers helpful guidance for this approach to the SoTL lit review. After analyzing 18 SoTL articles, they found 74 percent of the 954 in-text citations to be "non-substantive": either not connected to the article's argument or presented with "little importance, significance, or contribution to the theme, analysis, or results of the citing article," and "typically made without additional comments or context" (2020, 7). Each of the articles also cited these non-substantive references more often than any of the sources they used substantively. Their implications are clear, if understated: "SoTL literature reviews could often benefit from more depth" (12–13).

There are two common ways you can represent your lit review with depth. Let's start by thinking at the macro level, or about the paper or presentation as a whole. When you're ready to present your inquiry, you'll choose how and where to integrate your lit review. You have two options:

1. You may use the traditional IMRaD structure of scientific articles with predetermined sections for the Introduction, Methods, Results, and Discussion, and your lit review will appear in the introductory section (Healey, Matthews, and Cook-Sather 2020).

2. Perhaps you prefer something more organic and free-form that follows a narrative, an argument, or some other kind of unfolding of your inquiry, using sections and subheadings of your choosing. In this format more typical of scholarship in the humanities, you'll weave the existing research throughout the article to establish the relevant connections as they emerge, capturing the sense of an ongoing conversation.

In either case, you'll present your lit review fairly early in your article, illustrating the initial "they say" move that describes the existing conversations you're situating your "I say" within, harkening back to Graff and Birkenstein's "moves that matter in academic writing" (2021). Later in the article, you'll connect what you find in your inquiry to earlier studies or relevant parts of existing conversations. To illustrate, we've highlighted the lit reviews in a couple of articles: Yuen Fook Chan, Gurnam Kaur Sidhu, Narasuman Suthagar, Lai Fong Lee, and Bee Wah Yap (2016) follow the IMRaD format to report on a study on collaboration, feedback, and self-efficacy in a Malaysian university, and Stephen Bloch-Schulman (2016) uses a free-form approach to explore using think-alouds in a philosophy course in the US. Neither of these is better than the other but rather a matter of style and how you choose to present your work.

You can also create depth in the product of your lit review by tending to Cappello and Miller-Young's distinction between substantive and non-substantive citations. Rather than listing multiple citations in parentheses after a general statement or at the end of a paragraph, you can be explicit about these scholars' contributions to your work. For instance, when authors express a significant point effectively, quoting their language uplifts their work. And perhaps you're focusing on inquiry-based learning and want to intentionally build upon a few studies (e.g., the articles in table 5.1) for a specific purpose, such as highlighting how yours is complementary in presenting a different country, discipline, type of institution, or perspective. And perhaps a different paper (e.g., the one by Archer-Kuhn, Lee, Finnessey, and Liu 2020) provides the conceptual framework for the survey you use for your project. As you write about these articles, making these connections explicit speaks to the intentionality of your inquiry, the depth of your lit review, and the significance of what you find. By asking yourself, "Why did I find this person's work meaningful, helpful, or relevant to my own?" and then clearly representing this influence in the product of your lit review reflects a generous approach to scholarship.

We hope this chapter has helped you feel confident in both the process and product of your SoTL lit review. We also hope it has helped you recognize that, even if this is your first SoTL inquiry, you have something to contribute to SoTL. Your SoTL project—indeed every SoTL project that's shared broadly enough—becomes part of the ongoing conversations in Burke's parlor, where we're all trying to learn from each other.

Questions for You

We invite you to explore these questions in individual reflection or collegial conversation:
- How does your discipline engage with research literature? What aspects of your training and scholarly practice can help you engage with SoTL literature? How might you need to develop new practices or revise existing ones to engage with SoTL literature?
- What SoTL conversations do you want to listen—and to contribute—to? Why? Where do these conversations take place?

- What parts of the lit review process are most interesting—or most concerning—for you? Why?
- What kind of products do you hope to emerge from your SoTL inquiry?

Supplemental Materials

- Worksheet: Mapping Your Literature Review
- Reading: Two articles illustrating different (yet excellent) approaches to literature reviews, highlighted by Nancy, Peter, and Katarina to help you see how the article authors use their lit reviews. For an IMRaD approach to the lit review, look at the highlighted portions of: Yuen Fook Chan, Gurnam Kaur Sidhu, Narasuman Suthagar, Lai Fong Lee, and Bee Wah Yap (2016). For a more free-form approach to the lit review, look at the highlighted portions of: Stephen Bloch-Schulman (2016).
- Video: Janice Miller-Young, an engineering scholar, discusses how she approaches a SoTL literature search in this video (6:25) produced by the Center for Engaged Learning
- Video: Olivia Choplin, a scholar of French literature, explains how she approaches a SoTL literature search in this video (8:13) produced by the Center for Engaged Learning.
- Video: Margy MacMillan, a SoTL librarian, offers guidance on searching for SoTL literature in this video (10:43) produced by the Center for Engaged Learning
- Worksheets: These online resources for the book *Writing about Teaching and Learning* include prompts for writing in diverse SoTL genres and templates for responding to reviewers

CHAPTER 6

Relational SoTL Ethics

"...education is ultimately and immediately about an encounter between persons." —Michael Fielding (1999)

SoTL not only should be engaged with and contribute to scholarly conversations, but it also must center the people involved in the teaching, learning, and inquiry. The processes of SoTL are deeply human—asking questions, joining conversations, making meaning. The purposes of SoTL also are distinctly human — improving teaching, enhancing learning, changing institutions and communities.

The work academics do with students is complex, dynamic, important, and—as Fielding suggests in the epigraph above—fundamentally relational. Just as who we are shapes our teaching (and our SoTL), students' identities and motivations influence their learning. The connections between and among students and teachers can either enable or constrain learning (Bovill, 2020; Felten and Lambert, 2020). SoTL appeals to many academics because it provides both a framework and community for thinking carefully about the human connections at the heart of learning and teaching. These relationships also are central to ethical considerations in SoTL.

Teaching is full of ethical choices about fairness, integrity, care, and more. For instance, you establish a foundation for ethical behavior and decision-making in your syllabus policies about, say, the use of generative Artificial Intelligence in coursework. Ethical issues also can emerge in the moment, such as when a student in crisis asks for a major change in those policies to accommodate their particular needs. And broader ethical considerations include how to balance your own academic freedom to teach what and how you choose with both the needs and preferences of your students and also the curricular and professional standards established by your peers. Higher education scholar Bruce Macfarlane (2004) calls these—and many more teaching decisions—the "messy" choices that reflect "the real-life, everyday moral dilemmas that confront university teachers managing relationships with students and their colleagues" (1).

The ethical complexities of teaching multiply when you engage in SoTL. If your inquiry is within your own teaching context (as is most often the case), your relationship with your students takes on an extra dimension. Philosopher Gil Hersch (2018) explains, "Once teachers decide to evaluate an educational method they consider implementing, they introduce an additional goal to their classroom besides getting students to learn as best they can" (10). In this shift, although you're primarily their teacher, you're now also a researcher of their learning, and these two roles don't always align. Consider how some research practices would be ethical in many large scale studies but potentially perceived as unfair to students in classroom-based SoTL:

- As a *researcher*, for example, you might want to randomly divide students in one of your classes into two groups, providing one with an intervention you believe is educationally beneficial (e.g., a specific active learning experience) and providing the other a control condition (e.g., a traditional lecture). Many studies are designed in this way.
- As a *teacher* you might decide not to conduct a SoTL inquiry this way because, even if you judged this design to be ethical as a researcher, the randomly assigned groups—one of which withholds what is probably an educationally beneficial experience—could negatively affect the learning, performance, and autonomy of some of your students, and could be perceived by students (and others) to be unfair (Bunnell, Felten, and Matthews 2022).

Different academic teachers will balance such potential role conflicts differently, but we urge you to carefully consider how your SoTL inquiries might influence your relationships with students, as well as interactions among students. If your SoTL project has the potential to negatively influence learning or relationships in your course, you should either reconsider your plans or proceed with care and transparency.

You may be thinking that all of this concern about the ethics of your SoTL inquiry is unnecessary because you're a good person, and you care about your students. You would never put them in a risky situation, and you would certainly never cause them harm or try to coerce them to do something inappropriate. You strive to be fair in your assessment practices and professional in your relationship with students, so this chapter may even feel a little insulting. We—the authors of this book, the wider SoTL community, and colleagues who oversee institutional ethics approvals—don't mean to imply anything about you specifically or to doubt your good intentions. Instead, this vigilance about ethics emerges from the undeniable difference in power between *any* teacher-researcher (including you) and their students. As the one with most of the power, you need to be deliberate in trying to understand how students might experience that power, regardless of your intentions.

Some scholars have even wondered if *not* doing SoTL also has ethical implications. If we make decisions about teaching based primarily on our gut instincts or stories from colleagues, we are far more likely to act on misunderstandings of our students (Cox 2011; Poole 2018; Popovic and Green 2012) and on pedagogical traditions and assumptions that would not survive critical scrutiny (Nelson 2010). Indeed, STEM education scholars in the US have documented how active learning can close pre-existing equity gaps in student learning and performance in a course (Theobald, Hill, Tran, et al. 2020) and have raised questions about the ethics of continuing with purely didactic lectures when active learning has been demonstrated to be consistently more effective (Freeman, Eddy, McDonough, Smith, Okoroafor, Jordt, and Wenderoth 2014). At its core, SoTL inquiry is one evidence-informed way for academic teachers to improve their teaching and their students' learning. As Lee Shulman (2001) argued in SoTL's very early days, academic teachers have both an "individual and a communal" obligation to systematically enhance their own teaching and to contribute to the shared work of teaching in their discipline and in higher education (3). So, perhaps, doing SoTL—or at least being informed by SoTL—is one component of being an ethical academic teacher.

Practicing ethical SoTL is no less important than asking meaningful questions and situating your work within broader conversations, but there are a couple of reasons why we wrote this chapter a little differently than the previous two. First, the rules and policies for ethical human subject research vary based on national guidelines, institutional policies, and cultural context, so external advice goes only so far. Next, plenty of resources out there will guide you through the specific decisions you'll need to make to develop a SoTL inquiry that meets the ethical mandates of this kind of research. (See box 6.1.) For these reasons, we chose to focus here on our North Star of ethical SoTL: centering relationships. This means that this chapter will help you think through broader ethical implications of your SoTL inquiry. These involve not only reducing risk and ensuring that you can share the results of your inquiry – traditional concerns of research ethics – but also tending to your relationship with students. Additionally, taking a relational approach to SoTL ethics will enhance the design of your inquiry by centering what and who matters in this work. Below, we explore two key ethical touchpoints in SoTL: planning and sharing your inquiry.

Touchpoint 1: Planning Your SoTL inquiry

In your day-to-day work as a teacher, it's hard enough to see the needs and perspectives of each of your students. Fold in your additional obligations as you conduct SoTL inquiry, and things can get murkier. For this reason, as you begin to plan your SoTL project, take time to think through how students might experience your inquiry.

Many SoTL scholars begin by talking with colleagues. You could have a conversation with a SoTL-active colleague,

BOX 6.1

Do I Need Ethical Approval to Do SoTL?

The short answer is "Yes," at least in most higher education systems. As you saw in chapter 1, going public with your work is a fundamental aspect of SoTL, and to be able to share your SoTL inquiry with colleagues, you need to operate within the research ethics guidelines that apply in your context. This often means seeking ethical approval from your institution. In fact, some journals now require proof of this approval because SoTL typically falls under the umbrella of "research on human subjects," which is tightly—and rightly—regulated around the world, focusing on the ethical imperative of minimizing risk for the "human subjects" (or what we in SoTL might call "participants" or "students"). Since the rules and policies are so localized, you'll want to talk to colleagues and carefully consult the relevant documentation to find out what applies in your specific context.

Engaging with the formal ethics approval process can be enlightening and rewarding, and it also can be frustrating and demoralizing. Based on his longtime experience of chairing an ethics committee at a university in the US, Ryan Martin explains that applying for ethical approval "sometimes feels overly detailed, too subjective, unnecessary, and unfriendly to SoTL" (2018, 62). If you want to dig more deeply for the kind of practical guidance you'll need for gaining ethical clearance, we encourage you to talk with your institution's research ethics staff for tailored guidance and with SoTL-active colleagues for SoTL-specific guidance. (If you don't know them, ask at your academic development unit or teaching and learning center.)

someone in your campus's teaching and learning center, or another colleague whom you trust to serve as a critical friend who is both supportive and willing to ask challenging questions (Baskerville and Goldblatt 2009). One of the many reasons why these preliminary conversations are helpful is because you can ask these colleagues to listen to your ideas with the ethics of your relationships with students in mind. You might prime them with questions like the following:

- "Where in this plan am I—and where am I not—treating my students with respect and care?"
- "In my plan, are there points at which I seem to lose sight of my role in supporting student learning and well-being?"
- "Is there something here you think a student would object to?"
- "Given the inherent power in the teacher-student relationship, where, how, and/or when should I step back and invite someone else in (e.g., to collect consent forms from students) or delay until I'm no longer their teacher (e.g., analyzing their written responses for my inquiry)?"

These colleagues can draw on their experiences and understanding of the complexities of the teacher-student (and now teacher-researcher-student) relationship.

You're probably already thinking about our next recommendation. If colleagues are great partners in planning your inquiry, then students are (in some ways) even better. Imagine talking with a current or former student, or a group of students, about your inquiry—why you started, what you're wondering, how you're thinking about conducting it—and asking them the questions above.

Let's go even further. Students as Partners is a major movement in SoTL, emerging naturally from the field's approach to students and the relationship between teacher-researcher and students. Imagine partnering with a student from the very first step of your inquiry, such as the reflections in chapter 2 or the entry points in chapter 3, and then developing a meaningful question together in chapter 4, and so on. This collaboration doesn't guarantee an ethical, relationship-centered SoTL inquiry, but it places the perspective of a student and learner right beside you throughout the process (Bunnell, Felten, and Matthews 2022). Michelle Yeo and Cherie Woolmer (2022) invite SoTL scholars

---

BOX 6.2

SoTL Partnership with Students

"Students as Partners" (or "SaP") in SoTL is a natural extension of the field's approach to students and the relationship between teacher-researcher and students. To learn more, here are a few places to start:
- A foundational text is *Engaging Student Voices in the Study of Teaching and Learning* by Carmen Werder and Megan Otis (2009). You can watch their introductory video.
- A more recent book, edited by two (then) students and available online, is *The Power of Partnership: Students, Staff, and Faculty Revolutionizing Higher Education* edited by Lucy Mercer-Mapstone and Sophia Abbot (2020).
- *International Journal for Students as Partners* (*IJSaP*) is a journal devoted to this work.
- This video (10:38) on "Best Practices for Integrating Student Voices in SoTL" features Alison Cook-Sather, Mick Healey, Sophia Abbot, Hayley Burke, Huipu Li, Roselyn Appenteng, Alicia Walker, Carmen Werder, and Kara Yanagida, and was produced by the Center for Engaged Learning.

to consider the teacher-researcher role "as an opportunity rather than a problem to be solved," because it invites such partnership with both peers and students as you design and conduct your inquiry (39). To learn more, see box 6.2.

Touchpoint 2: Going Public

Centering your relationship with students will help you in making some key decisions as you go public with your SoTL inquiry. Sharing your work with others is typically the point at which ethical approval is required, and for good reason. You might be presenting examples of student confusion, misunderstanding, vulnerability, or even failure. Your ethics committee, colleagues, and especially students can help you honor students' rights to have their work and their identities treated with respect and care.

Think about how you'll talk and write about your students. First, deciding whether to keep student work anonymous isn't as simple as it seems. On one hand, you may think, "Of course, I'll anonymize everything!" Indeed, in order to protect students' identities when shared publicly, student work is often presented in aggregate or, if presented individually, with pseudonyms. But Mary E. Burman and Audrey Kleinsasser (2004) advise SoTL practitioners to let "students control the way their work is used," honoring their "ownership" of their own work (74). Defaulting to anonymity, they explain, means that students won't be attributed or applauded for their insights (which raises other ethical questions), so they advise asking students whether they want their work attributed to them by name. When Mariolina Rizzi Salvatori and Patricia Donahue (2005), literary scholars in the US who bring their field's high value on authorship, went public with their inquiry on reading difficult texts, their "Acknowledgements" section lists their students by full name, thanking them for "their graciousness in letting us cite their work" (xviii). Individual names also appear in the subheadings of sections that feature case studies of their writing. Additionally, Peter has used a two-step consent process before naming students, giving each person to be quoted the opportunity to read each quote in context before agreeing to their name being used in print (Felten and Lambert 2020). We're not advocating for this level of identification in all SoTL inquiries, and anonymity may make the most sense in yours, but we encourage you to consider talking with your students about it and giving them some choice.

Next, consider how you'll talk and write about your students if the learning hasn't gone well. As we pointed out in chapter 3, some SoTL projects begin as inquiry into "problems," such as students' inadequate or incorrect prior knowledge. A natural companion to Hutchings's *What works?* SoTL question is *What doesn't work?* As you can imagine, how student work is framed in these situations could, even if inadvertently, embarrass or shame students. Particularly in presentations, informal comments can come across as disrespectful or dismissive of students who are struggling to learn. (We've even heard audience members laugh at examples of student work presented at conferences.) To avoid this unintentional result, remind yourself—and your audience—that confusion, mistakes, and failure are not only expected in the learning process but are also part of the human experience. We're privileged that some students trust us enough to share such vulnerable moments with us, so we should treat them with care. A simple way to do this is by trying to connect back with the students in your inquiry to discuss your work before you present or publish. Even if they're not interested in your conclusions, they'll feel respected by the process.

Let's consider a couple of examples. Salvatori and Donahue (2005) not only name their students but also include extended passages in which these students describe their confusion about something they're reading. How, then, do the authors write about these quotes in ways that demonstrate respect for their students? After quoting a student, they begin their analysis of the students' work with framing comments like the following:

- "The first point we want to make about Funkhouser's response is that what she notices about the poem is *indeed worth noticing*." (21)
- "This is the response of a reader who has grown considerably over a period of a few weeks…." (26)
- "What can we learn from Stamm's work?" (32)
- "Both these readers single out as a difficulty the poem's unclear references; they do not know what certain words are referring to…. They are quite right. A writer's use of unfamiliar language can often make a reader feel that a work is inaccessible or impossible to understand." (40)
- "Pontoski states at the end that she still feels very confused about the poem. And yet, her writing displays a great deal of understanding." (42)

And there are more. In these moments immediately after a student quote, Salvatori and Donahue write with generosity, empathy, and respect for the student. That's an example of ethical, relational SoTL.

Another example comes from Tom Drummond and Kalyn Shea Owens (2010), education and chemistry instructors, respectively, at North Seattle Community College in the US. Their SoTL inquiry focused on how small groups of students work together to understand a difficult concept in introductory chemistry. With permission, they video-recorded student groups in action and then transcribed the recordings. Drummond and Owens then created a "capture" of key moments in the group work, centering what students do as they encounter something they don't fully understand (162). By concentrating on critical times in the group conversation, this inquiry reveals the very human processes of learning. Notice how they describe these moments (including the students' names) in the passage below:

> In the [capture] we saw how [students] Matthew, Melissa, Shana, and Kathryn were being powerful and capable. We saw how their learning did not proceed in a linear way but in fluid and tentative wandering. We saw how the construction of knowledge was a group process where each was nurtured by the conjectures and responsiveness of others—some confirming, others questioning—toward new connections and understandings. We saw how each person had unique contributions, pace, and strategies. (Drummond and Owens 2010, 181)

This approach to "listening more deeply" (182) to students as they struggle is another example of ethical, relational SoTL that centers empathy and care in the process of analyzing and going public with an inquiry.

As you move forward with your SoTL inquiry, think about how you'll tend to your relationships with students. Talking with colleagues, sharing your work with your students before you go public, and even fully partnering with students are great ways to help you design ethical, relationship-centered SoTL. These practices, and others like them, will also help you always remember that the heart of this work is "ultimately and immediately about an encounter between persons" (Fielding 1999, 22).

Questions for You

We invite you to explore these questions in individual reflection or collegial conversation:

- Beyond SoTL, what are your experiences with human subjects research? How could your approach to SoTL ethics be informed by—or perhaps challenged by—these other experiences?
- When might your dual role as a teacher and a SoTL-researcher be in tension? What can you do to manage that?
- How can you design your SoTL inquiry processes to be both caring and transparent for the people involved?
- How will you go public with your SoTL inquiry that honors and respects the people and ethics involved?

Supplemental Materials

Video: Several students and faculty offer recommendations for integrating student voices in SoTL in this video (10:38) produced by the Center for Engaged Learning at Elon University.

CHAPTER 7

Designing Your Inquiry

So far, section 2 of this book has guided you in reflecting on the teaching and learning issue you'd like to better understand, the kinds of questions you might ask, the literature that should inform your inquiry, and the ethics of your dual role as both teacher and SoTL inquirer. To explore the terrain of SoTL project design, this chapter will describe and illustrate two overarching SoTL designs aligned with Hutchings's *What is?* and *What works?* questions (2000, 4). The chapter also includes a possible step-by-step outline for an inquiry with both of these two questions.

Our attention to project design focuses on these question types for a couple of reasons: (1) as we pointed out in chapter 4, they're the most common, and (2) projects that can be categorized as "visions of the possible" and "formulating new conceptual frameworks" are typically *designed* as comparisons based on some kind of intervention or descriptions of something that happens—so their inquiry design tends to mirror either *What is?* or *What works?* (2000, 4–5). At the same time, we don't want to oversimplify these two designs: as you'll see in the variety of examples we share, there's room for great variation within each, and they support a diverse range of SoTL inquiries and SoTL scholars. They also aren't the only possible ways to organize your project. You don't need to follow in others' footsteps, but you also don't have to reinvent the wheel.

Before we dig in, we want to briefly return to one of SoTL's foundational metaphors to frame our approach to project design.

Designing for "The Trading Zone"

This stage of developing a SoTL project is a good time to revisit a persistent challenge in SoTL. Stephen Bloch-Schulman, Susan Wharton Conkling, Sherry Lee Linkon, Karen Manarin, and Kathleen Perkins (2016), humanities SoTL scholars from the US and Canada, have shown that "even from the beginning, SoTL had a conflicted relationship with its own intellectual diversity" (109). In "The SoTL Space" section in chapter 3, we described SoTL's tenet of welcoming contributions from across the disciplines, creating a vibrant and diverse "trading zone" of insights, perspectives, methodologies, and practices (Huber and Morreale 2002, 73; Mills and Huber 2005). Yet this variety also can be vexing because most of us are trained in disciplines that not only have traditions and practices for conducting research, but also are rooted in deep (and sometimes implicit) beliefs about the nature of knowledge and reality—what some scholars call ontology, epistemology, paradigm, or worldview (Miller-Young and Yeo 2015; Berenson 2018; Haigh and Withell 2020; Steiner n.d.). This diversity means that you'll likely encounter "alien epistemologies, methodologies, and concepts" as you engage in SoTL (Simmons,

Deshler, Kensington-Miller, Manarin, Morón-García, Oliver, and Renc-Roe 2013, 12).

To honor the inherent exchange in the "trading zone" of SoTL, we encourage you to bring an open and curious mindset to the project designs and methodological choices you and others make. If you find yourself having a negative initial reaction (e.g., you might think "an exploration of a single student's writing is not rigorous" or "all of these statistics are incomprehensible"), pause and take a few minutes to reflect. What assumptions about knowledge, learning, and research are guiding your SoTL inquiry? What might those assumptions enable you to understand, and what might they constrain? As Bloch-Schulman, Conkling, Linkon, Mandarin, and Perkins (2016) explain:

> If SoTL is to engage faculty across the disciplinary spectrum, it must embrace all kinds of research, including focused, controlled studies that yield statistical analyses and projects that tell significant stories about student learning and that emphasize interpretation, process, creativity, and theory. SoTL would be more inclusive, more interesting, and more significant if, rather than attempting to enforce methodological conformity, we recommitted to the original ideal of disciplinary diversity and exchange. (110)

You may not always feel you have firm footing in the varied terrain of SoTL. We certainly don't. That can be unsettling, but it's also exciting. Mel Hamilton and Brett McCollum (2024) urge SoTL scholars to lean into this discomfort by being explicit about the epistemological and ontological traditions that undergird our inquiries; doing that, they suggest, will help us understand what is actually happening in the SoTL "trading zone."

Ultimately, the methodological and epistemological diversity of SoTL supports a creative culture of teaching and learning (Fanghanel 2013) that not only helps each of us become better teachers, but also enables more (and more varied) questions and actions on the meanings and purposes of higher education, expanding what Booth and Woollacott (2018) call the "horizons" of SoTL to include the disciplinary, professional, cultural, and political.

Designing a *What is?* Inquiry

To Hutchings, *What is?* SoTL projects aim "not so much at proving (or disproving) the effectiveness of a particular approach or intervention but at describing what it looks like, what its constituent features might be" (Hutchings 2000, 4). This kind of analysis produces what some qualitative researchers call a "thick description" that offers rich contextual and observational details (Geertz 1973, 310). The power of a *What is?* inquiry does *not* come from generalizability, but rather from "representing complexity well" (Poole 2013, 141), or the way it represents learning and context in nuanced ways (Huber and Hutchings 2005; Chick 2024). These projects can take many forms, but most begin with a simple and humbling realization: as a teacher, I don't understand what my students think, know, or do in a specific situation (or perhaps more broadly). Let's look closely at a few examples so these ideas aren't so abstract.

What Is? Example 1

Johannes Bester and Eric Pretorius (2022) asked *What is?* in a large-enrollment, first-year civil engineering module on concrete technology at a university in South Africa. Recognizing that "pure content dissemination and recall is no longer sufficient" in engineering education, they weave together experiential activities and guided reflection designed to help students cultivate "employability skills and professional attributes that include skills for new knowledge generation, application of knowledge, values, and reasoning abilities" (111). Bester and Pretorius analyze individual writing by nearly 200 students to better understand the characteristics of "deep" and "shallow" reflection in their context, using literature and theory on reflection to guide their analysis. Their study allows them to better see—and then teach to students—the characteristics of deep reflection in civil engineering, which prepares students to thrive at university and as professionals.

What Is? Example 2

Unlike Bester and Pretorius's larger study of 200 students in South Africa, Holly Hassel and Joanne Baird Giordano (2009), who taught writing at a college in the US, did a smaller study of fourteen first-year students but used a more complex project design. They focused on what they describe as an "often-ignored student population": new undergraduates who don't demonstrate the critical writing and reading skills necessary to be placed in the required university-level writing course (25). Since these students couldn't graduate without passing this course, Hassel and Giordano wanted to better understand where these students struggle at the end of the first-semester preparatory writing course to better support them before they moved on to the required course.

To explore this question, they designed their project to use the course writing rubric to analyze all fourteen students' final papers from one preparatory class (see Phase 1 in figure 7.1). This process surfaced a general pattern, but not enough information to satisfy them, so they shifted to an in-depth analysis of three students' final papers from the first-semester preparatory course and first papers from the second-semester required course (see Phase 2 in figure 7.1).

Phase 1 revealed that most of the fourteen students wrote with "an incomplete understanding of academic writing conventions" (34), which would set them up to struggle in a subsequent required writing course and later when they write in future courses across disciplines. Phase 2 revealed the specific student difficulties of using conventions of formal writing, developing an informed argument (rather than summary and opinion), and engaging directly with readings from their own research. This careful, close attention to student writing mirrors the authors' disciplinary work of closely reading texts and allows them to make specific and important observations about *what is really happening*

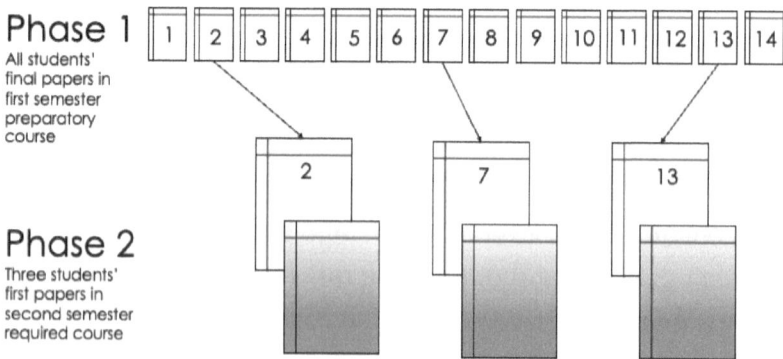

Figure 7.1. Hassel and Giordano's project design. *Phase 1*: Use course rubric to analyze final papers by all fourteen students in first-semester writing course: Where did they do well, and where did they still struggle? *Phase 2*: Closely read three students' final papers in the first-semester course and then their first papers in the second-semester required course: In addition to Phase 1 questions, what writing skills did they transfer to the second course? Adapted from Hassel and Giordano (2009).

with these students. The project's complex insight demonstrates the power of such exploratory, descriptive inquiries designed to get under the surface of students' learning—and also to offer clues about how academic teachers might adapt their pedagogy to support deeper, more enduring student learning.

What Is? Example 3

To explore a *What is?* SoTL question in multiple national contexts, Jennifer Hill, Kathy Berlin, Julia Choate, Lisa Cravens-Brown, Lisa McKendrick-Calder, and Susan Smith (2021) designed an inquiry at relatively similar (in size and mission) universities in Australia, the UK, and the US, exploring undergraduate students' emotional responses to instructor feedback on their course work. The project team used semi-structured small group interviews with twenty four students and, separately, six student-authored reflective journals responding to prompts like those asked in the interviews. They coded these qualitative sources to identify themes, finding perhaps most significantly that, across contexts, "feedback is taken personally by students"—even if that feedback is focused on the work rather than the person—and that this emotional interpretation of feedback influences a student's learning experiences in and beyond the course (301). They also found that "feedback evokes strong emotions in students at all levels of undergraduate study, across multiple subjects, and irrespective of the national regulatory environment in which the institutions are seated" (310). Like many other *What is?* inquiries, by digging into students' experiences, this project has implications for teaching and assessment in diverse contexts (311–313) even though it does not reveal—or attempt to understand—*what works*.

. . .

These three examples illustrate the basic outline of a SoTL project design that explores *What is?* Of course, the design of each project is complex and often evolves over time, but at some level *What is?* projects tend to have a rather simple, perhaps even elegant, design:

1. Begin by identifying something related to student learning that matters and that you want to understand more deeply. There are many possibilities for this "something." Looking back at your SoTL entry points (chapter 3), you may start with a curiosity, a problem, an aspect of students' prior knowledge, a belief about their learning, something specific to your context, some variation among students, a gap in existing research, or one of your commitments.
2. Think about what you want to know about this "something," and develop your SoTL question (chapter 4). If you want to know what this "something" looks like, you're in the right place. Consider how your question is—or could become—meaningful, as well as how you can make it more precise to your context (i.e., *when, where, for whom*).
3. Situate your inquiry within the relevant literature (chapter 5) to clarify and sharpen your question, and to identify the approach and activities that will help you answer your question (i.e., your methods).
4. Critically reflect on the ethical considerations of your project (chapter 6).
5. Identify the relevant learning experiences or moments that will answer your question (e.g., comments in a specific in-class discussion, responses on a quiz or paper).

6. Gather examples of student work that can be used as evidence or artifacts that help you answer your question (chapter 8 will guide you through this step).
7. Analyze student work in a way that responds to your question, using your own disciplinary training and the relevant scholarly literature as a guide (chapter 9 addresses your analytical approach).
8. Reflect on what you've learned through this process. How is it meaningful, helpful, and important to you, to students (yours and others'), to colleagues (near and far), or perhaps beyond any educational institution?
9. Turn your reflections into a contribution (chapter 10)—both to yourself, by applying what you've learned in your teaching, and to others by sharing with your colleagues and students.

Designing a *What Works?* Inquiry

The other question that also sets up a common SoTL project design asks, *What works?* Pat Hutchings (2000) notes that, "not surprisingly, this is where many faculty begin seeking evidence about the relative effectiveness of different approaches" of teaching because problems of practice so often motivate SoTL (4). She also underscores that *What works?* questions almost always have "a ready audience, an element much to be wished for in this and other forms of scholarship," since it promises to offer concrete guidance on how to be more effective (4).

What Works? Example 1

Victoria Holec and Richelle Marynowski (2020) wanted to understand whether the physical classroom at their university in western

Canada influenced student engagement with active learning. They build on deep literature about the efficacy of active learning, and also on their own experiences of teaching in classroom spaces that are more or less conducive to this pedagogical approach. Because Marynowski was scheduled to teach two sections of the same course in two very different rooms (one designed as an active learning classroom and one configured as a traditional lecture theatre; see figure 7.2), they decided to conduct a *What works?* inquiry comparing the two. Marynowski also taught both sections the same term, so she could ensure the course design, her teaching approaches, and the context of the course were essentially the same, making the classroom space a salient distinction between the two learning experiences. Their inquiry revealed that "learning environment matters to achieve improved results for student-perceived engagement" (154). They found that

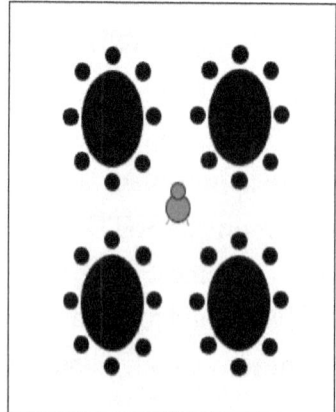 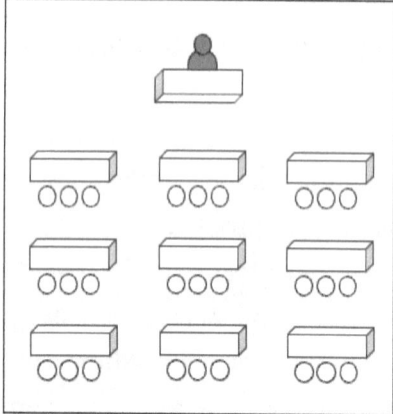

Figure 7.2. Holec and Marynowski's project design. The teacher, the course design, teaching approaches, and context are essentially the same (gray); the students and the physical classroom are different (black and white). Adapted from Holec and Marynowski (2020).

student-perceived engagement was also relatively high in the traditional lecture classroom, underscoring the significant influence of the course design, instructor, and pedagogy no matter the physical space; however, they also found that the active learning classroom made a real difference in self-perceived engagement reported by the students and the instructor (155). In short, this inquiry shows that in this context, teaching with active learning *works* better (as measured by self-perceived engagement) in a classroom designed for that pedagogy.

What Works? Example 2

Rather than inquiring into student perceptions, Holly Swanson, Adelola Ojutiku, and Bryan Dewsbury (2024) ask a *What works?* question about student metacognitive behaviors at a US research university. Metacognition, or the ability to accurately assess one's own understanding, has been shown to be crucial for student learning and success in higher education. More than 1,000 undergraduates at this university participated in a workshop designed to cultivate their metacognitive study practices. All workshop participants then had the opportunity to join a four-week online program that "scaffolded, reflective opportunities to extend the impact of the workshop" (4). Swanson and her coauthors gathered qualitative and quantitative data from the more than 200 students who completed the program, comparing them to some 160 students who began but didn't complete it. They "found a correlation between completing the intervention and a higher semester GPA [Grade Point Average], regardless of student identity, prior academic performance, [or study] strategy choice" (12). In other words, at a basic level, the four-week online program *works*. Yet the differences between "completers" and "non-completers" might primarily be linked to the level of student motivation overall, so those differences might simply highlight the importance of motivation. To unpack that possibility, Swanson, Ojutiku, and Dewsbury analyzed their data further and discovered that, regardless of motivation, "completion of the multiple reflective opportunities can improve student academic success across all student identities" (13), suggesting that the metacognitive behaviors practiced in the four-week program matter for all students.

These two examples illustrate the basic steps of a *What works?* SoTL project design. At a high level, the steps to develop these projects parallel *What is?* as the design of each is complex and often evolves over time, but the nature of a *What works?* question changes how you implement each step:

1. Begin by identifying something related to student learning that matters and that you want to understand more deeply. There are many possibilities for this "something." Looking back at "Where to Start" (chapter 3), it can be a curiosity, a problem, an aspect of students' prior knowledge, a belief about their learning, something specific to your context, some variation among students, a gap in existing research, or one of your commitments.

2. Develop your question by considering what you want to know about this "something" (chapter 4). For *What works?* questions, you're probably looking for some kind of change, or demonstration of effectiveness, or some other comparison. Don't forget to consider how your question is—or could become—meaningful and how you can make it more precise to your context (i.e., *When?*, *Where?*, *For whom?*).

3. Situate your inquiry within the relevant literature (chapter 5) to clarify and sharpen your question, and to identify the

approach and activities that will help you answer your question (i.e., your methods).
4. Critically reflect on the ethical considerations of your project (chapter 6).
5. Identify the relevant comparisons that will answer your question (e.g., between "completers" and "non-completers" in a course, between students this term and students in a prior term).
6. Gather examples of student work that can be used as evidence or artifacts that help you answer your question (chapter 8 will guide you through this step).
7. Analyze that student work in a way that responds to your question, using your own disciplinary training and the relevant scholarly literature as a guide (chapter 9 addresses your analytical approach).
8. Reflect on what you've learned through this process. How is it meaningful, helpful, and important to you? to students, yours and others'? to colleagues, near and far? perhaps beyond any educational institution?
9. Turn your reflection into a contribution (chapter 10)—to yourself by applying what you've learned in your teaching and to others by sharing with your colleagues (and with your students).

Designing Your Inquiry in Context

Now that we've sketched the broad contours of the two most common SoTL project designs, let's get specific to your inquiry. At this point, revisit your plan and make sure you've articulated the particularities of your context by responding to those crucial modifiers *where?*, *when?*, and for *whom?* Put even more simply:

- If you're designing a *What is?* project, you're really asking *What is here?* and *What is with these students?* and *What is now?* Take a few moments to write some notes on where here is, who these students are, and when now is.
- If you're designing a *What works?* project, you're really asking *What works here?* and *What works with these students?* and *What works now?*, so write some notes on where "here" is, who these students are, and when "now" is.

These elements of your inquiry's context matter, which is one reason why we include relevant aspects of context for the SoTL projects we describe and cite. A SoTL inquiry might have broad implications, but it is by definition rooted in a place and time involving people in cultural and institutional contexts. You'll want to remember these contexts as you conduct your project and as you share your work.

We hope the examples and guidance above help you design a SoTL inquiry that responds to what you want to know and that the variety of sample studies in the sections above illustrates the range in size, scope, contexts, and more that are welcome in SoTL's "trading zone." The next chapter will help you plan to collect the "traces of learning" that will be at the heart of your inquiry.

Questions for You

We invite you to explore these questions in individual reflection or collegial conversation:
- Do you and your disciplinary peers tend to design research projects that look more like *What is?* or *What works?* What do you see as the strengths, and the weaknesses, of that kind of SoTL question?

- Try reorienting your inquiry with a different starting question—if your question currently is *What works?* then try *What is?* or *What if?* What do you notice about your question—and your inquiry—when you start with a different kind of question?

Supplemental Materials

- <u>Worksheet</u>: Designing Your Inquiry
- <u>Video</u>: Three faculty describe diverse examples of SoTL projects in this video (5:00) produced by the Center for Engaged Learning

CHAPTER 8

Collecting "Traces of Learning"

Your inquiry design process has prepared you for the next step in SoTL, gathering and analyzing data, evidence, or artifacts that help you respond to your question. This can be the most exciting, the most important, and sometimes the most time consuming part of the process as you carefully collect and explore what Karen Manarin calls "traces of learning" (2017, 168; more on this shortly). To do more than simply confirm your expectations, this phase of your inquiry needs to be as comprehensive, systematic, and transparent as possible. You also need to be open to surprising, perhaps even troubling findings. We'll guide you through this phase, but first a few thoughts on terminology.

A Word about Words

You might notice that in SoTL conversations and writing there's not a consensus on what to call the information at the core of an inquiry. You might encounter *data* and *evidence* most frequently, and you might even hear people using those terms interchangeably. Language matters, so we'd like to dig into these words briefly.

Data

Data is a common term in some research fields and often is used for the raw, uninterpreted information SoTL practitioners collect from and about students. For example, in an international survey of research approaches used in the SoTL literature, Aysha Divan, Lynn O. Ludwig, Kelly E. Matthews, Phillip M. Motley, and Ana M. Tomljenovic-Berube (2017)—working in the UK, Canada, Australia, and the US—employ the word "data" to describe all quantitative and qualitative information being analyzed in these inquiries. This use of "data" is familiar to scholars in many disciplines, so it can serve as a helpful shorthand when communicating about SoTL with peers in those disciplines.

Data, however, is not our preferred term, in part because it doesn't acknowledge that people—students, usually—are the creators of that information. We believe that using a somewhat less common word might help us all be more conscious about the ways SoTL is always about people acting in the world.

Evidence

Evidence is another common term in SoTL. Randy Bass and Sherry Lee Linkon (2008), for instance, emphasize the importance of using "evidence of student thinking and learning" in SoTL, rather than relying on "generalizations about student learning, based on the lived experience of the teacher" or "more general speculations about how students will necessarily respond" to specific situations (255). The term *evidence*, which they describe as "the 'visible action' of student learning," prevents us from relying on faulty assumptions about what students are thinking and learning—or not (Bass and Linkon 2008, 258; Popovic and Green 2012).

Like the word *data*, in the SoTL literature the term *evidence* typically is used broadly, without any assumptions of a specific type or form of information. Our hesitation with using this word in SoTL inquiries is that, unlike the more generic *data*, *evidence* is inherently connected to a specific claim, hypothesis, or belief. In other words, returning to Bass and Linkon, SoTL inquiries investigate "evidence *of* student thinking and learning" (254; emphasis added). A presumption of what will be found is baked into the language: the collected evidence will show whether students have learned what was expected. But SoTL inquiries sometimes surprise us, creating what Michelle Yeo, Karen Manarin, and Janice Miller-Young (2018) describe as "breakthrough insights about teaching, learning, research, and themselves in a community of academics" (27). They contend that in SoTL, "we must allow ourselves to be surprised, caught off guard, brought up short" (19), so perhaps the term *evidence*—while useful in many contexts—carries some risk because it directs our attention towards what we *expect* to see, rather than what is *actually* there, or the question we emphasized in chapter 4, *what is really happening here?* Also, for a non-native English speaker like Katarina, the word *evidence* often is related to attempts to prove something, something that may not be possible.

Artifacts

That is why we have come to favor the term *artifact*. Karen Manarin, a literary and SoTL scholar whose disciplinary perspective leads her to think deeply about questions of authorship, prefers this word for its association with things "students create," things that are "shaped by a series of choices the student made ... in a particular time and context" (Manarin 2018, 102). This act of creation, she explains, leaves "traces of learning," rather than definitive "evidence" that students did or did not perform to our expectations (Manarin 2017, 168). As she suggests, *artifact* connotes an archaeological sense of objects that are imprinted with the thoughts or actions of people within a specific time and place, and that are available for analysis outside of that specific time and place. Artifacts can also include a range of forms and formats, such as informal or formal student writings, answers to exam questions, oral presentations, comments in class discussions that are captured through observation, or recorded performances. In short, *artifact* has the benefit of describing many student-created (or teacher-created) materials, yet it doesn't carry with it the risky assumptions of *evidence* referred to above. It also emphasizes that what we're studying is work done by people—that is, particular people in a particular setting—reinforcing the contextual nature of all SoTL inquiry.

We will use *artifact*, as well as Manarin's accompanying phrase "traces of learning," in the remainder of the chapter and the book. We want to be as expansive and inviting as possible, while also staying true to some of our key principles. For instance, this language elevates the humans at the heart of this work and the importance of who, where, and when they are. The language of "traces" also broadens our field of inquiry in a way that reflects SoTL's expansive view of learning, inviting us to collect things that give us insight into students' learning experiences and processes—including what and how they're thinking before they get to the stage of *having learned something*, or not—as well as the diverse experiences that inform who they are as students.

How We Make Meaning from Traces of Learning in the Trading Zone

As scholars, our disciplines offer a powerful lens for making meaning, and we've spent a long time developing and refining our use of that lens. This often—and appropriately—informs our inquiries into teaching and learning, creating what Huber and Morreale (2002) called the "disciplinary styles" of SoTL (see also chapter 2). These differences might be most evident in our SoTL inquiries in how we gather artifacts and make meaning from them through our analyses. In fact, in their "trading zone" metaphor for SoTL, these approaches to gathering artifacts and making meaning are among the "wares" that "scholars from different disciplinary cultures come to trade" (73).

At the same time, this diversity also presents certain challenges that are not always as salient within our disciplines, where shared methodologies and epistemologies are understood and practiced. This common ground is what makes a discipline. Yet since SoTL isn't a single discipline but instead brings together many disciplines to work toward shared goals (see chapter 1 and chapter 7), the field embraces different ways of making meaning. The result is that if you're new to SoTL, you might wonder if there's a right way to frame an inquiry, specific artifacts that should be collected, or a particular way to analyze them. Underlying these questions is a deeper one about certain disciplinary approaches and methods being more acceptable or rigorous than others. These kinds of questions sometimes leave new (or even experienced) SoTL scholars feeling that they don't have sufficient knowledge and expertise to conduct or share an inquiry.

We believe a little scholarly humility is helpful in reminding us of the limits of what—and how—we know. There's no single or *right* way to make meaning from artifacts of learning. Academia is made up of many approaches to creating knowledge, what knowledge means, and what creating this knowledge means. This diversity of disciplines and approaches is a hallmark of higher education—and of SoTL.

We also believe that the SoTL community is made up of many colleagues who are stretching and growing, brought together by our interest in postsecondary teaching and student learning. We encourage you to see your disciplinary background as a strength in your SoTL. Rather than focusing on your methodological gaps ("If only I had more expertise in this other approach!"), we invite you to lean into the assets your disciplinary training brings to a SoTL inquiry. We also hope you will welcome the perspectives and insights of colleagues who have very different approaches from yours. The disciplinary styles of SoTL make us stronger.

Principles for Collecting Artifacts as Traces of Learning

No matter the term you use or the ways you make meaning, your SoTL inquiry will involve collecting artifacts. To go beyond hunches, intuition, and lore (Poole 2018), you need to look for and at traces of learning. How will you decide what to collect and analyze? We offer four principles to guide your decisions in table 8.1 (also see the Collecting Your Artifacts worksheet in the Supplemental Resources section of this chapter).

Principle 1: Use Artifacts that Are Relevant to Your SoTL Question

The first principle is perhaps obvious, but it merits emphasis because SoTL inquiries can flounder by being overwhelmed with

Table 8.1. Principles for collecting artifacts as traces of learning
Use artifacts that are relevant to your SoTL question.
Use artifacts that make traces of student learning visible.
Use what's available.
Use a variety of artifacts.

too many or less relevant artifacts. You need to be selective and focused, and a guiding principle should be alignment between an artifact and your question (Mueller 2018).

Consider, for example, what a high grade in a course demonstrates. The student who earns such a mark surely has generated traces of learning related to all of the course's goals. For some SoTL inquiries, these diverse traces might be significant. But if you're curious about how students make sense of complex readings (see the example from Salvatori [2000] below for more on this), then an overall course grade probably is not a relevant artifact for your inquiry because it is too broad. To avoid this kind of misalignment, use these two questions to guide your selection of artifacts:

- What traces of learning does this artifact make visible, precisely?
- What traces of learning does it *not* make visible?

This principle can be seen clearly in a 2022 article by Chwen Jen Chen and Chi Siong Teh. Chen and Tech noticed that, with the emergency transition to remote instruction at the start of the COVID-19 pandemic, they could no longer observe student learning behaviors in the classroom at their university in Malaysia. To better understand their students' experiences in the online context, Chen and Teh set out to gather digital artifacts of student-instructor, student-student, and student-content interactions. They used the course's learning management system and records from a course-associated virtual messaging app to capture artifacts of these interactions. Since Chen and Teh aimed not only to document students' learning activities but also to explore students' thinking that informed course behaviors, they surveyed all of their students and conducted interviews with active, moderately active, and passive students in the course. The artifacts they collected and the conclusions they drew aligned with their goal of "discover[ing] students' unseen online interaction behaviors and experiences in order to obtain insights into ways to devise relevant online pedagogical approaches" (1). Chen and Teh report on students' preferences, affective responses, and external barriers to develop "insights into commendable pedagogical practices" that would enhance interactions with course content, the instructor, and other students (16). They do *not* offer conclusions about the effect of these behaviors on students' learning. If Chen and Teh had set out to make claims about the effect of certain online behaviors on student learning, they'd have needed to collect and analyze different artifacts, which would have been a much different inquiry. As readers of their work, we admire the crisp alignment between their SoTL questions and their artifacts.

Principle 2: Use Artifacts that Make Traces of Student Learning Visible

As we emphasize throughout this book, meaningful SoTL inquiries can focus on students' acquisition of core disciplinary knowledge and skills, or they can explore a range of related topics including students' emotional or social experiences in a course—both of which can profoundly influence learning. The artifacts you collect should provide traces of learning that make visible to you the aspects of students' learning experiences at the heart of your inquiry. This might include final products of student work like essays or exams, but sometimes earlier work (e.g., drafts, lab notebooks, homework, discussions, and more) can be more meaningful, depending on your inquiry. Randy Bass and Bret Eynon (2009) underscore the importance of "making student thinking visible" by looking to "artifacts that captured the intermediate and developmental moments along the way," rather than just at the end products of the learning process (9). These artifacts, which are often forgotten and "left on the cutting room floor" (16), can be rich and full of meaning in ways that speak directly to your question.

Mariolina Salvatori (2000), who you saw using students' real names in her inquiry in chapter 6, illustrates Principle 2 in an inquiry that makes visible some typically invisible moments in the learning process in her discipline. She wanted to understand what happens when her students at a university in the US read challenging texts in her literature course, so she developed the Difficulty Paper, a brief ungraded writing activity that captures students' struggles with the demands of reading by asking them "to identify something difficult in a text and describe, in detail, why they experience it as difficult" (85). As part of her inquiry, these short writings offered a glimpse into each student's thinking process as they read, including where and why they struggle and potentially what they *don't* know—all information not available in their final essays, which tend to present confident explanations of what they *do* know as the result of a completed reading process that often also includes class discussion and instruction on that reading. Salvatori's inquiry illustrates the value of looking at artifacts that reveal what's happening when students are still developing their learning, including when they struggle with concepts and skills. Such a focus can lead to a SoTL project that provides guidance on how to help students navigate difficult moments in learning. In fact, one way Salvatori has shared this guidance is directly with students, through her textbook co-authored with Patricia Donahue, *The Elements (and Pleasures) of Difficulty* (2005).

Like Salvatori, Camille Kandiko, David Hay, and Saranne Weller (2013)—all at a university in the UK—sought to explore what's often a "lost opportunity to engage with students while they are developing their understanding," so they adopted concepts maps to "externalize" students' development of "personal learning" (72). Their SoTL inquiry focused on how students reflect on and make their own sense of course material before they started to write a final paper. In their article, Kandiko, Hay, and Weller (2013) closely analyze this trajectory in one student's concept maps at the beginning, middle, and end of a classics course (75–77; see figure 8.1, next page). By examining three artifacts of learning from the same student, the authors are able to trace over time the increasing complexity of this student's understanding of the course's core concepts, documenting the intermediate steps that not only reveal a great deal about this student's learning journey but also suggest implications for adapting and using concept maps to surface students' thinking processes—to themselves and their teachers—in other humanities courses.

Principle 3: Use What's Available

Conducting a SoTL inquiry doesn't necessarily require you to develop new ways of collecting traces of student learning. Before

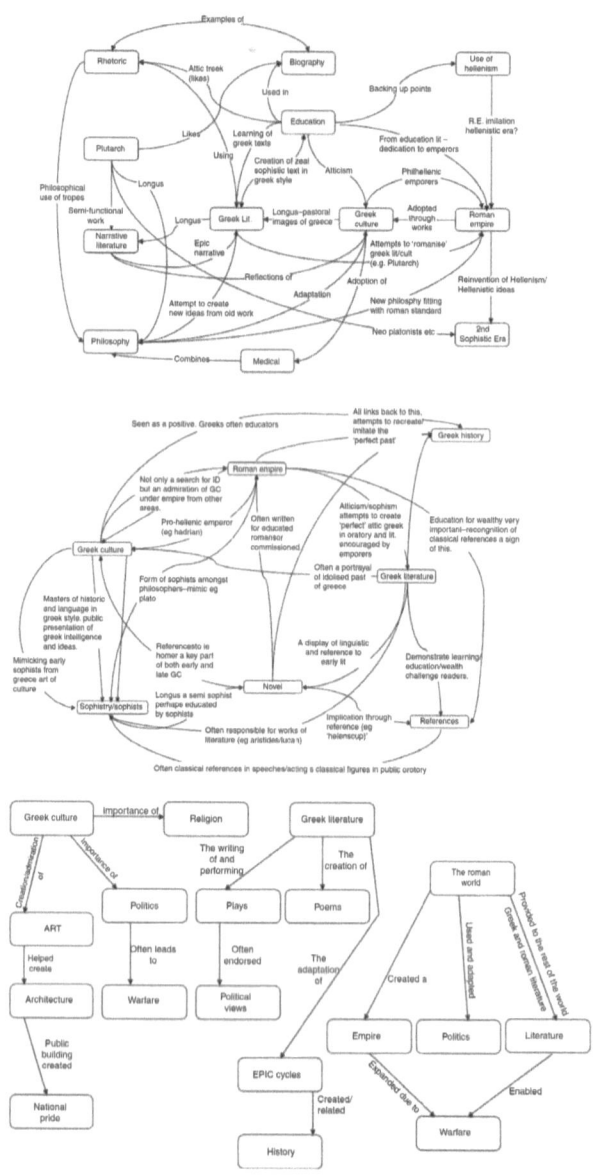

Figure 8.1. The traces of learning of one student throughout the semester. Reprinted by permission of SAGE Publications. Camille Kandiko, David Hay, and Saranne Weller, "Concept Mapping in the Humanities to Facilitate Reflection: Externalizing the Relationship between Public and Personal Learning," *Arts and Humanities in Higher Education* 12(1): 70–87. Copyright © 2013 by SAGE Publications.

you start to invent anything new for your inquiry, look at the materials students already create as part of the regular work of a course, such as written drafts, lab reports, problem sets, discussion board responses, calculations, quiz results, and exam answers. As student learning activities, these artifacts probably capture lots of important learning moments, and drawing from these already-available materials can keep a SoTL project simple, doable, and not too time-consuming—as long as they provide traces of learning relevant to your SoTL question. Keep in mind, though, that using students' course work also can raise ethical questions that require careful attention (see chapter 6.) Also, if you use these materials in your inquiry, you're probably looking at something more specific than the overarching learning assessed in the course, so using existing student work will require you to revisit those materials to analyze them through the lens of your inquiry, a process that's distinct from grading that work.

For example, to compare students' historical thinking at the beginning and end of an introductory history course at a liberal arts college in the US, Lendol Calder and Robert Williams (2021) focused on the formative assessment activities Calder already used in his teaching. In these activities, students reviewed historical sources and responded to specific questions that also prompted them to "explain the reasoning behind their answers in a few sentences" (11). Calder routinely collected these responses as part of the class, so gathering the artifacts didn't change his (or his students') workload at all during the semester. Analyzing the artifacts with Williams after the course ended (to avoid the ethical complications of simultaneously grading and studying students) was new work, of course, but this inquiry helped Calder better understand his students' evolving historical thinking skills, knowledge that he and Williams then shared in an article published in one of his discipline's premier scholarly journals.

Available artifacts aren't limited to assigned course work, though. As described under Principle 1 above, Chen and Teh (2022) used analytics available in their learning management system, the course's social messaging app, and other digital tools to gather artifacts related to their students' virtual interactive behaviors, and then supplemented these with surveys and interviews to better understand how their students experienced these interactions. Sometimes institutional data about students, informal or optional course activities, and other artifacts can be analyzed in your inquiry, in combination (or not) with course specific materials. Following the principle of "use what's available" does *not* mean you're limited to what's already at your fingertips, but it does encourage you to start there.

This principle also underscores the importance of ethically collecting and storing artifacts of student learning. SoTL inquiries often involve gathering artifacts from students during a teaching term, with analysis taking place only after the term has ended. If your inquiry follows this design, then you need to plan ahead to ensure you have appropriate artifacts available when you turn your attention to analysis.

Principle 4: Use a Variety of Artifacts

A final principle for effectively identifying artifacts for your SoTL inquiry is to aim for variety. As we've noted in previous chapters, student learning is complex, and drawing on multiple types of artifacts will more fully represent this complexity, especially when they offer complementary (or perhaps contradictory) information. Social science researchers sometimes refer to this approach

as "triangulation," or the attempt to gather diverse artifacts by "critically considering the explanatory capacity of" each (Cousin 2009, 115). In other words, as you consider each artifact closely, revisit the guiding questions from Principle 1:
- What traces of learning does this artifact make visible, precisely?
- What traces of learning does it not make visible?

Your answers to these questions will help you choose an effective variety. In the previous example, Chen and Teh (2022) illustrate this well by blending quantitative counts from online course tools with qualitative comments from surveys and interviews. Not every SoTL inquiry needs to use such a diverse array of artifacts, but often you can better answer your question or deepen your inquiry by considering complementary artifacts. Table 8.2 lists many (but not all) of the kinds of artifacts that commonly are used in SoTL projects.

In listing these, we're not suggesting you should use all of them, or that you should only consider artifacts included in this incomplete list. Instead, we invite you to start by brainstorming as many relevant artifacts as possible for your inquiry and then, after critical reflection based on the principles above, concentrate your analysis on the ones that seem most salient in relation to the SoTL question you are exploring. The more traces of learning you have, the more confidently you can make sense of what you are seeing.

At the same time, we also encourage you to remember that more isn't necessarily better. As you've seen above, Chen and Teh (2022) used an appropriately wide array of artifacts aligned with their question, while Salvatori (2000), Kandiko, Hay, and Weller (2013), and Calder and Williams (2021) concentrated on just one type of artifact that speaks to their questions. Sometimes

Table 8.2. Sample SoTL artifacts that make visible different traces of learning

Types of Artifacts	Examples of This Artifact
Samples of students' regular work in the course	papers, journals, lab notebooks, projects, presentations, performances, recorded or online discussion, exam question(s), reading quizzes
Snapshots of students' thinking	minute paper, muddiest point, preconception check, concept maps, problem sets, clicker/polling data, reflective journals, reading annotations, difficulty papers, observed in-class comments
Artifacts of learning processes	think-alouds, multiple drafts of the same student paper/project,, observed/documented in-class behaviors over time, student created (or co-created) rubrics
Probes of what students think	surveys, interviews, focus groups
Behavior measures	online postings, office visits, pages read/written, hours spent studying
Institutional research data	grade point averages, placement exam scores/rates, admissions numbers, retention rates, campus scores on national survey data (e.g., US National Survey of Student Engagement)

in SoTL, using less—while also going deeper in your analysis, as seen in these examples—is more. So rather than worrying about the *quantity* of artifacts you use in your inquiry, we encourage you to focus on the *quality*. Artifacts that are relevant, that make thinking visible, that are available, and that are diverse will provide a strong foundation for any SoTL inquiry.

Questions for You

We invite you to explore these questions in individual reflection or collegial conversation:

- This chapter begins with commentary on *data*, *evidence*, and *artifacts*. Which of these terms are most familiar to you? Which seems most useful to you in SoTL? Why?
- Thinking about your SoTL inquiry, what artifacts are most relevant to your question? What traces of learning do these artifacts reveal? What other "traces" might you need to find or uncover?
- What artifacts are already available for your use? Do you need to develop any new ones?
- How could you add variety to the artifacts you use in your inquiry? Or, perhaps, how can you simplify your inquiry so you are using fewer artifacts by focusing only on the most relevant ones?

Supplemental Materials

Worksheet: Collecting Your Artifacts

CHAPTER 9

Analyzing Artifacts Systematically

After gathering your relevant artifacts, it's time to begin analysis to explore *how* these artifacts respond to your original SoTL question. This is a sense-making activity in which you'll carefully view these materials through a new lens. Specifically, for your SoTL inquiry, you're setting aside the teacherly perspective of grading student work or assessing it according to specific course learning goals (unless those goals are the focus of your inquiry). Instead, you'll look at these artifacts from a different perspective, exploring with a scholarly mindset what they reveal about the questions at the heart of your SoTL inquiry.

Some disciplines use the word *methodology* for the meaning-making process of analyzing artifacts, but other disciplines don't. In this section, we aren't going to describe a single SoTL methodology (as you've seen, there are many because of the diversity of the field and we intentionally want to acknowledge that), nor are we going to tell you how to carry out any particular methodology, for the same reason. Instead, this chapter offers principles and guidance for analyzing your artifacts no matter which methodologies you use.

Some SoTL inquiries draw on prior research or existing theories and conceptual frameworks (e.g., how learning happens, how people interact, disciplinary competencies, people's emotions, power dynamics) as ready-made tools for identifying meaningful patterns in the collected artifacts. Recall table 5.1 in [chapter 5](), where you saw similar projects that draw on very different conceptual frameworks (i.e., Vygotsky's Sociocultural Theory, Self-Determination Theory) to analyze their collected artifacts. And in [chapter 8](), Kandiko, Hay, and Weller (2013) explicitly build on three foundations for their analysis of concepts maps in a classics course. First, they frame their inquiry with scholars who study learning, underscoring that "measuring change in understanding is genuinely difficult" because that change is internal to a person (72). This leads them to concept mapping as a well-researched process for making thinking visible, allowing for analysis of change over time (72–73). Finally, they explain why the most commonly used methods for making meaning from concept maps (a quantitative approach developed in the sciences) aren't sufficient to make sense of the kinds of learning they see in the humanities, so they draw on theories of reflection and transformation to supplement their methodology (73–74). These three strands of research and theory provide a robust basis for their analysis.

There are also plenty of SoTL inquiries that analyze the collected artifacts inductively (that is, without drawing on preexisting frameworks or expectations) in equally systematic approaches. Ingie Hovland (2021) describes her inquiry process that unfolded as she encouraged her religion students at a university in the US how to "read in discipline-specific ways" (1). As she analyzed responses to nine "writing to read assignments" (29) in which students chronicled their reading processes, she "repeatedly returned to the question: *What is happening when students read before class?*" (emphasis in original; 29). In her her article, she tracks each of her steps through this process, repeatedly returning to metacommentary about her thinking as she applied this question to student work. In many ways, her article reads like she's doing her analysis as we read, a meticulousness that documents her careful work of meaning-making.

Systematic SoTL Analysis

Whether your approach is deductive (i.e., using an existing framework to guide your analysis) or inductive (i.e., allowing the analysis to emerge from the artifacts), your choice and application of your analytical process should be *systematic*. We prefer the term *systematic* to *rigorous* because the word *rigor* has very specific meanings in some contexts (e.g., the US National Institutes of Health (n.d.) defines scientific rigor as the "strict application of the scientific method to ensure unbiased and well-controlled experimental design," particularly in the context of reproducibility in research) and has been hotly contested in teaching and learning in other contexts (e.g., Supiano 2022). Also, the etymology of *rigor* implies stiff, rigid, and inflexible, which are distinctly not part of our vision for SoTL. While *systematic* might seem restrictive to some colleagues, our intention is to emphasize that your approach to analyzing artifacts should be based in a system that guides you in making meaning. Being systematic will help you (and others)

Table 9.2. Principles of systematic SoTL analysis
Be *intentional* in choosing your analytical approach.
Be *methodical* in applying the approach.
Be *careful* with each step.
Be *receptive* to unexpected results and insights.
Be *connected* throughout your process.

feel confident that what you're finding through your analysis is not simply reinforcing any prior assumptions about student learning or your teaching. Being systematic, however, does *not* require you to follow a rigid step-by-step protocol. Of course, some disciplines have clear, specific methodologies for analyzing artifacts, and those might be appropriate in your inquiry. But other disciplines approach meaning-making more inductively by carefully implementing iterative, reflective, or creative processes, and those might be right for your inquiry. Every SoTL inquiry should have (and explicitly describe) a system for its analysis, but we invite you to decide on what that system might—and should—be in your inquiry by revisiting your responses to earlier chapters in this book. Indeed, your SoTL question surely could be explored with diverse methods, depending on your motivations for doing SoTL, your chosen entry point, your disciplinary background, and more. We encourage you to embrace that variation while also recognizing that you should approach any analytical approach systematically.

In the previous chapter, we shared some guiding principles for collecting artifacts that offer traces of learning. Here, we offer the five principles of systematic SoTL analyses (table

9.2)—namely, that systematic analyses in SoTL involve being intentional, methodical, careful, receptive, and connected.

Principle 1: Be Intentional in Choosing Your Analytical Approach

You have choices to make about your approach, and you want to choose with intention. As you've seen in the example studies we've described, you might analyze artifacts through your specific disciplinary lens, through the lens of a relevant conceptual or theoretical framework, with an open and exploratory mindset, or in collaboration with colleagues who bring one of these lenses. Regardless of the approach you choose, be thoughtful about *why* you are doing what you are doing.

Principle 2: Be Methodical in Applying the Approach

As you draw on and then apply an analytical approach informed by your discipline, the literature, and/or experienced colleagues, document the choices you make and the subsequent processes or methods. This might feel like a lot of extra work, or you may think you can just do it later ("I'll just figure that out when the time comes!"), but investing your time to plan and describe your work will make analyzing your artifacts go more smoothly and will make explaining your choices much easier and more precise. Sometimes an inquiry's analytical approach can also make a contribution to SoTL by showing colleagues how they could walk a similar path. Recall, for example, Hovland's 2021 article that chronicled her analysis as if in real time. Her explanations help readers understand how she analyzed her artifacts and why she chose an inductive approach, while also showing what such a process can look like.

Principle 3: Be Careful With Each Step

Perhaps this goes without saying, but it's worth noting that a systematic analysis involves being deliberate not just in selecting your analytical approach and planning your analytical process, but also in implementing each step of that process. Carefully follow your plan while also periodically revisiting your original goals and your question to make sure what you're doing aligns with them. Also, since the artifacts you analyze are created by students, those artifacts—and the students behind them—deserve to be treated with care throughout the inquiry process.

Principle 4: Be Receptive to Unexpected Results and Insights

Although maintaining the above commitment to being intentional, methodical, and careful is important, you also want to be willing to explore surprising or disappointing results. After all, in SoTL, learning something about teaching and learning is more important than strict fidelity to your original plans. Recall, for example, Hassel and Giordano's (2009) shift from analyzing all students in one class to following three from that class to the next (chapter 7), and how Peter's SoTL inquiry (box 4.2) prompted him to change class exercises about reading visual sources in history. A surprising result in your inquiry can feel frustrating at first (it certainly did for Peter!), but unexpected findings can also be generative and exciting if you're open to them.

Principle 5: Be Connected Throughout Your Process

Finally, analyze your artifacts with an eye toward the connectedness of how scholarly knowledge is produced. Even if you're the sole inquirer in your SoTL project, you are not working alone. More specifically, just as you'll periodically reflect on the relationship between your process and your question and goals, you'll also want to reflect on the relationship between what you're finding and other humans relevant to your inquiry. For example, keep your analysis connected to what others have shared in relevant literature. As you recall from [chapter 5](), your work is part of an ongoing conversation with peers, so don't lose sight of being part of this conversation. Your work is also deeply relational in its responsibility to students ([chapter 6]()), so occasionally ask yourself how the students at the heart of your inquiry would react to what you're finding. You may have even chosen to work alongside others (e.g., colleagues or students as co-inquirers) to complement your analytical perspective and maintain an immediate (and even enjoyable) sense of connectedness.

This systematic approach to analysis in SoTL—that is, being intentional, methodical, careful, receptive, and connected in analytical practices—allows a diverse field like SoTL to be systematic in its methods while also embracing the diversity of people involved. It also distinguishes SoTL from more informal and ad hoc reflections on teaching and learning, which can be vulnerable to faulty assumptions, biases, or incomplete information.

Being Transparent about Being Systematic

As we explained in chapter 1, all SoTL involves going public by sharing your work with others. We'll say more about this in chapter 10, but for now, as you think about analyzing your artifacts systematically, it's important to be aware of your potential audiences in and beyond SoTL. This means you can't (or shouldn't) think of your audience as monolithic because they may be:

- SoTL colleagues who share your disciplinary background or those who come from disciplines that are very different from yours
- Peers from your institutional or cultural context or from a context far from yours
- Fellow educators and students or colleagues from your disciplinary community unfamiliar with SoTL
- Administrators, some of whom will be unfamiliar with SoTL, or even people outside of higher education who are unfamiliar with your teaching, your contexts, your discipline, and SoTL

For any of these audiences, you should be able to clearly explain your inquiry's artifacts, analytical processes, and guiding assumptions in a way that these audiences from different contexts will understand (Berenson 2018; Moore 2018).

This is particularly the case if you intend to share your inquiry in peer-reviewed settings like journals or conferences. You'll need to anticipate a range of expectations and practices in your audience, and then to be transparent (i.e., explicit, clear, and detailed) about the following choices:

- What artifacts you collected for your inquiry, and why

- How you systematically approached analyzing these artifacts, and why
- How you carried out that systematic analysis

This may also seem like a lot of unnecessary work, especially if you're used to sharing your work with colleagues in the same discipline. When we stay within our disciplinary community, we can often just use shorthand about our approaches and methods because we all typically come from a common intellectual tradition with a shared language. Moving beyond that community, however, requires us to make the tacit explicit. This requirement also applies when we share our SoTL work within our disciplinary community if we've adopted any approaches or methods from outside of that community. Both of these may seem vexingly difficult, but below we'll share three examples of such transparency, so you can see what it might look like.

An article by Brett McCollum, Lisa Regier, Jaque Leong, Sarah Simpson, and Shayne Sterner (2014) illustrates this transparency. Their inquiry, a large study of undergraduate general chemistry students in Canada, aimed to understand whether using touch-screen technology to manipulate representations of molecules positively contributed to the students' "spatial cognitive skills related to molecular geometries" (1810). In their article published in a major disciplinary journal, they explain their complex interview process in seven paragraphs and supplement it with a more concise visual representation (reproduced here in figure 9.1). Readers of this journal are primarily chemistry educators who are looking for rigor but don't use interviews as a disciplinary methodology, so the authors were especially attentive to showing how they were systematic in their inquiry. Specifically, their interview protocol included five steps, each timed and conducted in the same way to allow for comparison between a group of students using the touch-screen technology and those using paper-based images of the molecules. Although this method may not be familiar to disciplinary colleagues, the authors' explanation and accompanying graphic (2014, 1811; see also figure 9.1) make this complex but systematic process transparent to their readers.

Foong May Yeong also illustrates being transparent about the systematic choices she made for her SoTL project (2021). She analyzed her students' posts in an asynchronous online discussion forum as they collaboratively attempted to solve ill-structured

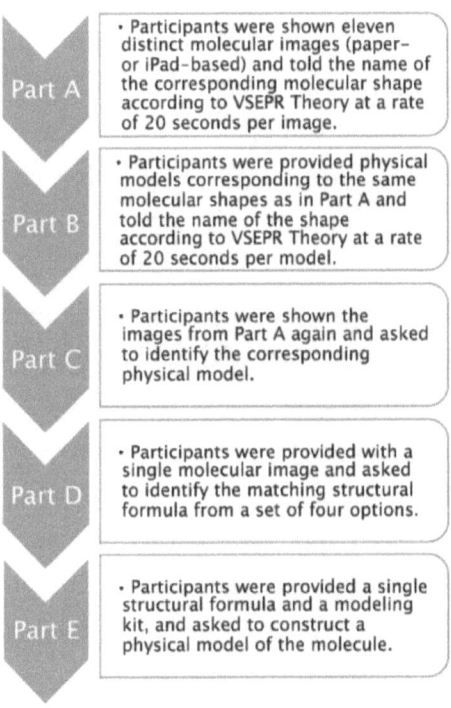

Figure 9.1. Transparent presentation of interview protocol.
Reprinted by permission from Brett M. McCollum, Lisa Regier, Jaque Leong, Sarah Simpson, and Shayne Sterner. 2014. "The Effects of Using Touch-Screen Devices on Students' Molecular Visualization and Representational Competence Skills," *Journal of Chemcal Education* 91(11): 1811. Copyright © 2014 by American Chemical Society.

problems in an upper-level undergraduate biochemistry course at a university in Singapore. In her article published in a multidisciplinary, international SoTL journal, Yeong is admirably attentive to the diversity of her readers. After describing her inquiry's foundation in existing research on problem-solving and in sociocultural theory (2021, 139–141), Yeong explains the mixed (both qualitative and quantitative) methods used to analyze this student work. Below are the steps she takes to be transparent:

First, she devotes three clear paragraphs to describing her qualitative approach (2021, 143–144): two about what she did ("the grounded approach" to content analysis), what it means, and how it's relevant to her inquiry, and then a third, jargon-free paragraph explaining exactly how she applied it to her artifacts:

> I first interpreted students' posts … as to what they were attempting to achieve during their exchanges and coded them … for common themes that emerged and collapsed similar themes together into … categories … [that] provided a better overview of students' problem-solving approaches without being overwhelmed by the numerous posts. (Yeong 2021, 143–144)

She also includes a table of the most frequent codes from her analysis (146), as well as all of her codes and categories in the article's appendix (158–161). Even further, she walks her reader through how she coded and then categorized posts that demonstrated a particular problem-solving move from the existing research (146–147). Yeong also explains the quantitative method used to analyze the students' posts (144). In a single paragraph she starts with the method she chose, how she applied it, and why (i.e., "Descriptive statistics, such as frequency distributions of students' posts across time, were used to understand broad tendencies of students when undertaking problem-solving tasks."), followed by stating that it complements her qualitative approach to respond to her inquiry (144). Yeong's transparency throughout these sections allows readers from a range of disciplines to follow and understand how she carried out her analysis.

For a final example, let's return to Karen Manarin (2016), our inspiration for "traces of learning" in this chapter, as we look at another article that effectively makes transparent choices about artifacts and analysis. She conducted a SoTL project on using posters in her upper-level literature classroom at a Canadian university. Manarin aimed for this poster assignment to accomplish some of the discipline's goals that are lost in the typical final research paper, including the "scholarly practice" of "interaction with texts and with each other" and "some of the cognitive, affective, and aesthetic aspects of literary research" (1). Like Yeong, Manarin published her work in a multidisciplinary, international SoTL journal, so she states at the outset:

> Even as I hope to influence my disciplinary colleagues' practices by providing the arguments and evidence that they will find convincing, I need to explain those practices and justify my methodological choices to those who do not understand how we create knowledge within the discipline. (Manarin 2016, 2)

She understands the need to be transparent. A little later, she explains, "I read closely, looking for patterns and creating my interpretations of student learning" (3).

When she gets to her analysis, Manarin does the following: She starts by articulating her surprise at what surfaced through these posters, demonstrating that she didn't bring a pre-existing framework for her analysis. She spends over six pages writing about five student posters and their accompanying reflections. This extended section *shows* how she read closely (including students' choices in "color palette, texture, and layout as well as textual or illustrative elements"), looked for patterns, and developed her interpretations of the student learning made visible in this project (6–12). She ends her article by explaining why she is transparent. First, she wants her disciplinary colleagues, her SoTL colleagues from all disciplines (including those who "may be suspicious of" her approaches), and the broader "higher education community" to understand the meaningful learning she sees in these students' posters (13). She also wants to ensure that her work is recognized as systematic by members of the SoTL community, who "do not have to agree, but they do have to consider an interpretation or approach seriously enough to enter into critical, and productive, conversation" (13).

These three examples of effective transparency for specific audiences offer some possibilities for your inquiry. You may use McCollum, Regier, Leong, Simpson, and Sterner (2014) as a guide by carefully describing your analytical approach and offering a succinct visual representation of it. Or you may follow Yeong's (2021) lead by more briefly describing your choices, but also illustrating your process with an example, and perhaps including your analytical materials (e.g., codes, interview protocol) when you go public. Or you may decide that you want to use Manarin's (2016) strategy of briefly describing the approach but then devoting a significant portion of your article (or presentation) to actually show your analysis.

Indeed, as Manarin suggests, the goal of this transparency isn't to teach readers how to adopt or practice an unfamiliar method. It's impossible to be *that* transparent in a few paragraphs or pages. We learn new methods by following citations, reading widely and deeply, pursuing extended study, or collaborating with others. Instead, this transparency in sharing our SoTL inquiries invites and enables our colleagues—regardless of who and where they are—to follow what we did and why, and to understand our choices in being systematic. This transparency will provide a strong foundation for the next step in your inquiry, sharing your work with others.

Questions for You

We invite you to explore these questions in individual reflection or collegial conversation:
- What does "systematic" mean in your disciplinary tradition? Can (or how can) your SoTL inquiry be both systematic and rooted in your disciplinary training?
- Which of the principles in this chapter feel most familiar—or unfamiliar—to you? Why?
- How might you be even more transparent in your SoTL work?

Supplemental Materials

Worksheet: Applying the Principles of Systematic SoTL Analysis

CHAPTER 10

Sharing What You Learn

Once you've analyzed your artifacts, you might be wondering what to do with what you've learned from that analysis—and from the entire process of conducting your SoTL inquiry. You might ask, *Is it worth the effort of going public? Will anyone care about my modest inquiry in my unique context? Do I* really *have anything to contribute?* To these questions, we say "Yes!" Sharing what you learn is not only a core step in SoTL, but it is a powerful opportunity to make meaning for ourselves and to build connections with others: "Writing can capture and convey what makes us human, what makes us connected, what keeps us alive" (Healey, Matthews, and Cook-Sather 2020, 17).

In this chapter, we'll share some of our reasons for this response. This chapter won't review all the possible venues and genres for going public because there are many of both available for your SoTL inquiry, and plenty of helpful resources exist to guide you in these choices (see table 10.1 near the end of the chapter), but we think the reasons for going public are more important and less familiar.

The 6 Ps: Why You Should Share What You've Learned

Lee Shulman (2001), who played a pivotal role in the early evolution of SoTL, offers three reasons to engage with SoTL as a scholarly endeavor that you make public, which he called the three Ps:

- *Pragmatic*: to improve our own teaching and our students' learning
- *Policy*: to influence practices and structures of teaching and learning in and beyond our institutions
- *Professional* obligation: to contribute to our academic community's knowledge of teaching and learning

We'd like to add to Shulman's list:

- *Purpose*: As chapter 2 emphasizes, your sense of purpose should guide your SoTL inquiry, including why and how you share what you've learned.
- *Participation:* We also want to bring forward chapter 5's metaphor of engaging in SoTL as joining a conversation. Participation in these conversations is an essential component of SoTL and a primary means of sharing your work.
- *Public:* Finally, contributing to these conversations is a public act that also aligns with Boyer's vision for a SoTL to enhance learning, teaching, institutions, and our world. To Boyer, SoTL is inherently public because it aims:

  not only to prepare [academic teachers] for productive careers but also to enable them to live lives of dignity and purpose; not only to generate new knowledge [about teaching and learning] but also to channel that knowledge to humane ends; not merely to study [teaching and learning] but to help shape [higher education institutions] that can promote the public good. (Boyer 1987, 119)

Figure 10.1 illustrates how our expanded list of six Ps builds on Shulman's original framework. We've explored Shulman's three Ps in earlier chapters (especially chapters 1, 2, and 3), and he's written at length about them, so this chapter will focus on ours.

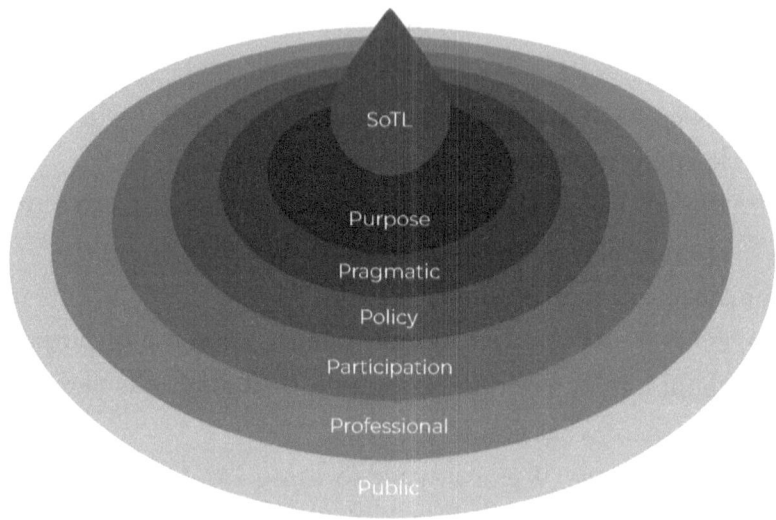

Figure 10.1. An extension of Shulman's Three Ps.

Purpose

Early in the book, we asked you to reflect on your SoTL purposes—and then to have your purposes guide your inquiry. We now want to extend that further.

We believe that sharing your SoTL work can reinforce your sense of purpose. Explaining to others *what* you do and *why* you do it can be empowering for you, and it can build community with others who have similar interests and commitments. Talking about *why* might feel uncomfortable if you're trained in a discipline that values objective research. (*Do I really need to talk about my purposes when I should be talking about my results?*) We encourage you to start with your purposes so that your colleagues can understand the foundations of your inquiry. We also believe that the modern academy has become so results-oriented that it obscures the meaning of our work. By starting with purposes, we aspire to create more human and humane ways of sharing not just the results of our work but the reasons why that work matters.

The results orientation in the academy (more, more, more!) has very human costs. Since the COVID-19 pandemic, burnout has been a significant problem in higher education globally (Flaherty 2020; Pope-Ruark 2022). But the pandemic isn't the sole cause. Indeed, Xueli Wang, a leading higher education scholar in the US, notes that "While some of the specific challenges were spurred by the pandemic, collectively, these issues are a reflection of longer-standing, deeper, and pervading problems around work expectations and norms, treating individuals as expendable, inequitable compensation, and demoralization" (2024, 130). For instance, looking beyond those who teach in higher education, much of the pre-pandemic research on burnout focused on nurses because their rates are among the highest globally (National Academies 2019; Woo, Ho, Tang, and Tam 2020). One of the many reasons for this is the gap between what nurses see as the most important part of their work (i.e., treating patients with an emphasis on quality and care) and the work they're compelled to do (i.e., treating patients with an emphasis on quantity and efficiency). The "moral injury" of this gap leads to, among other things, the feeling that their work not only lacks meaning and impact but also negates why they chose to be nurses in the first place (Stovall, Hansen, and van Ryn 2020). Although this research has rightly emphasized systemic change as the best way to mitigate this burnout, it also points to strategies individual nurses can use to see their work as meaningful, and to know that others see it as meaningful as well (Leiter, Harvie, and Frizzell 1998; Leiter and Maslach 2009). We believe academic teachers can learn from the research on nurses, and sharing our SoTL inquiry is one way to see that work as meaningful and to know that others see it as meaningful as well. This can also be an important way to develop and align our professional identities (Healey, Matthews, and Cook-Sather 2020, 32–42).

Our goal in writing this book is to guide you through a process of developing a SoTL inquiry that feels deeply informed by what matters to you (chapter 2 and chapter 3), meaningful (chapter 4), connected to others (chapter 5), caring (chapter 6), respectful of students' learning experiences (chapter 8), and more. When you share your SoTL inquiry with others and highlight any of these characteristics, you may be surprised (as we have been!) by the often warm reception to your work. These moments will remind you, often when you need it most, that your work has purpose.

Participation

Sharing what you learn from your SoTL inquiry also helps you participate in the ongoing scholarly conversations about learning and teaching, especially the ones that influenced you along the way (chapter 5). When you participate in these conversations, you not only add your voice, experience, and expertise, but you also have the opportunity to collegially shape them by inviting others in, guiding attention to questions that merit further attention, and building an even stronger community to sustain the conversation about this consequential work.

In writing about the ethics of SoTL, Ryan Martin (2018) observed that, by *not* going public with our SoTL work, "we miss out on an opportunity to do the most possible good" for "other teachers and future students" (67). You may recall that in [chapter 1](#) we described SoTL as *inquiry into teaching and learning for the purposes of improving teaching and learning in context and of contributing to what we know about teaching and learning*. The latter part of that declaration relates to the heart of this chapter, *what* we *know about teaching and learning*. That "we" refers to the communities that are typically the core conversation partners in SoTL: disciplinary colleagues, people in other fields on our campus, our students, and academics in other institutions and in other parts of the world. As we've written earlier, we in higher education have so much to learn about teaching, learning, and students. We need your SoTL work. Your colleagues need your SoTL work. Students—not just yours, but others' as well—need your SoTL work. By contributing in this way, all of us—individually and together—will better understand the complexities, the richness, and the possibilities of our teaching and students' learning experiences.

Contributing what you've learned doesn't necessarily mean publishing an article in a peer-reviewed journal. Michael Anthony Samuel, from South Africa, notes that SoTL practitioners' "publication," or their ways of going public, "could be translated in a variety of spaces," not just "the academic publications industry" (2017, 25). Indeed, SoTL inquiries are provisional, ongoing, and highly contextualized, so contributing to SoTL conversations in ways that honor these features is important. This aligns with one of this book's themes inspired by Gary Poole (2013): the aim of SoTL is *not* proving something is either true or universal, but rather our task is "representing complexity well" (141). In chapter 5's section on Identifying Your Contribution, you recognized how the particularities of your project (e.g., your context, your perspective, how you complement existing work) are among its strengths. When you share your work, lean into those aspects of your inquiry rather than downplaying them to meet the expectation, common in some disciplines, of making generalizable claims that apply across all contexts. (This is neither a realistic nor an appropriate goal for SoTL precisely *because of* the strength in particularities.) With this in mind, we again encourage you to approach sharing your SoTL inquiries as an opportunity to participate in the scholarly conversation captured in chapter 5's central metaphor of a parlor of discussion.

But we also invite you to take our encouragement literally here: participate in scholarly conversations about this work with colleagues. Katarina's research with Torgny Roxå (Roxå and Mårtensson 2009) has demonstrated that these kinds of "significant conversations" with trusted colleagues are foundational to academic teachers' learning and growth. These conversations are permeated by mutual trust, intellectual stimulation, and a generosity in supporting problem solving and challenging and encouraging ideas—all qualities that speak to SoTL in general, and to your SoTL. Such conversations often take place with close colleagues, but they don't have to. The SoTL community is spread far and wide, so if you can't find someone at your institution, there are plenty of conversation partners out there who'd welcome you. In chapter 12, we'll help you find some colleagues and communities that are eager for you to join their conversation.

Drawing on your SoTL inquiry to participate in these conversations (both metaphorical and literal) will also help you break down some of the isolation that academic teachers commonly experience, what Shulman (1993) called "pedagogical solitude" (6). At many institutions, the classroom is the domain of individual academic teachers, which can be positive when it allows for creative pedagogies; however, this tradition reinforces what Randy Bass (1999) has described as a reticence among many to talk about their struggles (or their successes) in the classroom. By sharing our SoTL inquiries, we are joining, contributing to, and building community by making ourselves and our work open to others. This is truly a "significant conversation." And when many of us contribute from our diverse perspectives and positions to SoTL conversations, we are nurturing a dynamic community that will in turn nurture us professionally. Teaching is hard work. Doing that hard work in community not only makes us more effective, it also has the potential to make the experience more rewarding and even more joyful.

Public

Finally, we want to revisit our earlier definition of SoTL to leave you with a challenge, or perhaps an inspiration. We describe one of SoTL's goals as *contributing to what we know about teaching and learning*, and we identify many of the audiences implied in that "we," including disciplinary colleagues, people in other fields on our campus, our students, and academics in other institutions and other parts of the world.

We also encourage you to think beyond these audiences. In chapter 1, we include the public good as one reason to do SoTL. In chapter 2, we list many reasons why you may choose to do

SoTL, including your own concerns about that public good. In chapter 3, we offer your commitments to some larger purpose as a possible entry point into a SoTL inquiry. In chapter 4, we appreciate Anthony Ciccone's (2018) claim that "meaningful SoTL questions," among other things, are "truly consequential" (17). You may be sensing a pattern. If any of these moments resonate with you, a final reason to go public with what you learned from your inquiry takes "public" a little farther.

Indeed, the "we" in SoTL's goal of *contributing to what we know about teaching and learning* is sometimes well beyond educational institutions. There have long been calls for SoTL inquiries that make the world a better place by focusing on how best to educate students to become good people and responsible citizens who support justice and equity (Booth and Woollacott 2018; Gale 2009; Kreber 2013; Leibowitz 2010; Scharff and Hamshire 2022). More recently, though, some SoTL scholars have called for us to mobilize SoTL-generated knowledge, or *what we know about teaching and learning*, to contribute to everyday moments

---

BOX 10.1

An Example of Public SoTL

To see an example of the result of a public SoTL project, visit toolsforsocialjustice.org. The tagline for this site is "SoTL-Informed Strategies for Everyday Interactions." Written as a jargon-free site for truly public audiences, it mobilizes some of the existing research on why students resist learning to frame some of the possible motivations for resistance to social justice, followed by SoTL-informed strategies for changing minds based on those specific motivations.

of teaching and learning (Behari-Leak 2022; Chick and Friberg 2022; Huijser, Seeley, and Cronin 2023). Consider that, on some level, teaching means changing people's minds, and learning means changing your mind. This notion of "public SoTL" challenges the SoTL community (including you) to think about what we know and how we can share what we know to support efforts to change minds *out there* in important, just, and necessary ways (Behari-Leak 2022, 35).

Take, for example, social justice. Social injustice is often rooted in how people think about difference (e.g., race, gender, socioeconomic class, nationality, language). How does this thinking develop? What actions can interrupt or change this thinking? How does thinking inform action? And so on. They could be—and are—SoTL questions. Some in the SoTL community are engaging with these issues already (see box 10.1), and you may be developing a SoTL inquiry that speaks to similar questions. (You may not, and that's okay, too.) If you are, you'll certainly want to share it in ways that reach relevant audiences in the public, such as people who want to help change how family members, communities, and even nations think about difference and social justice.

How to Share What You've Learned

Now that you see many reasons why you should share what you've learned by going public with your SoTL inquiry, let's consider how you might do so.

Torgny Roxå, Thomas Olsson, and Katarina Mårtensson (2008) have conceptualized two different trajectories in SoTL work. In Trajectory 1, the aim of sharing is to contribute to the teaching and learning culture in your department or at your institution. Trajectory 2, on the other hand, sets out to contribute to teaching and learning *beyond* the local by focusing on your broader discipline or even the international SoTL community. These two trajectories are not mutually exclusive—many people engaged in SoTL probably follow both of these trajectories (see box 10.2), whether at once or at different times. But the two trajectories are informed by different purposes, audiences, and expectations. Trajectory 2 tends to have more traditional academic expectations for formal, polished, and even sophisticated work, while Trajectory 1 can be a more comfortable and friendly environment for emerging inquiries. (We also want to acknowledge that Trajectory 2 can at times feel friendlier than some institutional contexts, so we don't want to oversimplify.)

What will *your* trajectory look like? Let's explore some possibilities. As you revisit your responses to the early chapters in this book, the answer to this question about your trajectory may become obvious. Your reasons for doing SoTL (chapter 2), your entry point (chapter 3), the meaningful SoTL question you developed (chapter 4), and the existing conversations you chose to contribute to (chapter 5) may imply a clear trajectory toward a particular audience and how to reach them. Let's say, for example, you did the following:

- You decided to reflect on your teaching in chapter 2 because you wanted to develop a SoTL inquiry to help you grow and change as a teacher.
- The entry point focusing on your beliefs in chapter 3 provoked you to think critically about some of your assumptions about how you teach. The entry point about variation led you to think specifically about how you teach students who are the first in their family to study in higher education.

BOX 10.2

One SoTL Trajectory

Ingela Johansson is a senior lecturer in Spanish at a research-intensive university in Sweden. With limited resources and time for teaching, she meets her students in the A-level class for only a few hours per week. Outside of that, students are expected to read a lot of literature and practice understanding and speaking Spanish. She and her colleagues often talk about how they don't think students spend enough time on their studies, and course evaluations indicate the same. Ingela decides to do a SoTL project. She asks her twenty-nine students to write a diary during one week of studies, and to note whatever they do that's study-related on each day of that week. She finds out that students actually spend much more time studying than she and her colleagues had thought, but also that they spend that study time on different things than she'd expected (e.g., spending more time reading Spanish texts than practicing speaking Spanish). Ingela revises her course and adds new practice exercises that students are expected to perform individually and in groups outside of class hours. These additional activities steer the students towards deeper and more purposeful learning and are positively evaluated by the students and Ingela as a teacher. She first presents the results of her SoTL inquiry to colleagues in her department, opening up new topics for their ongoing collegial conversations. Later, she presents her study at a local campus conference on teaching and learning, where teachers from a range of disciplines attend.

Because of the broad interest in her topic (what students do with their time outside of class and how teachers can influence that) and the encouragement she experienced at the campus conference, she wrote and published an article about it in a national journal (Johansson 2012).

- You then applied chapter 4's guidance by developing a SoTL question about how this specific group of students in your classes experiences the first few weeks of the semester when you're orienting students to your course. You started to wonder if you had assumed these first-in-family students knew what you meant by your foundational expectations, such as "read the assigned texts carefully" and "be prepared to discuss in class."
- As you listened widely and deeply, as suggested in chapter 5, you were drawn to the literature on equity-minded teaching, where you discovered the Transparency in Learning and Teaching (TILT) framework (Winkelmes 2023), which offers specific guidance on how to make explicit the expectations and assumptions of any assignment or activity (called TILTing an assignment). In these conversations, you find plenty of studies about many students, but not as many about first-generation college students and even fewer from your specific context, so you're eager to contribute what you learn about supporting your students in their first few weeks.
- The *What works?* project design in chapter 7 inspired you to TILT the first major assignment in an introductory course you teach and then compare the quality of student work on that assignment with student performance on a non-TILTed version of the assignment from a prior semester.
- Chapter 8 points you to specific artifacts, not only the students' work on that first assignment but also a process log, where students will chronicle some of their intermediate thinking as they work on this assignment.

This path of developing your inquiry may lead you to specific communities and connections that are new to you. Your own institution may host a teaching and learning conference each year, and you decide that this is the perfect place to share your inquiry for the first time. You also may find an organization with a significant focus on access and equity for first-in-family students, such as SPARQS in Scotland, the South African National Resource Centre, or the Gardner Institute in the US. Perhaps one or more of these organizations hosts an annual conference, or maybe another conference coming up has a relevant theme. And, of course, you'll know that you're enthusiastically invited to share your work at any SoTL conference near or far from you.

At some point, you may decide to stretch further by, for instance, writing and submitting an article to a SoTL journal, a journal focused on these particular students, or one of your field's relevant journals. (You can find a searchable database of SoTL and SoTL-friendly journals in the Teaching Journals Directory curated by the Center for Excellence in Teaching and Learning at Kennesaw State University, and shortly, we'll say more about the most intimidating part of submitting to a journal, peer review.) Or you may reach out to the host of a relevant podcast to share what you've learned (e.g., "60-Second SoTL" from the Center for Engaged Learning at Elon University) or write a post for a relevant blog (e.g., the ISSOTL blog). Your inquiry may even inspire you to create an infographic about your project or about its results and your recommendations (Keogh, Lowell, Laios, McKendrick-Calder, Molitor, and Wilbur 2024). Or you may want to put your work on social media (e.g., reaching out to Sarah Langridge to be interviewed for her "In A Spark" newsletter on LinkedIn). And so on.

You may also substitute some of the "or" conjunctions above with "and" because, more than likely, you'll end up sharing your work in multiple ways. Also, while all of this may sound very linear, and sometimes your experience will unfold in this way, we've often found that the path may be more circuitous. Your SoTL trajectory, then, may begin with your deliberate choices, as above, and maybe it will follow a clear plan, but be open to both serendipity (Green 2024) and surprise (Yeo, Manarin, and Miller-Young 2018).

Less formal settings (e.g., small conferences, posters at SoTL conferences, local seminars, podcasts, blogs, social media) are opportunities to share and receive feedback on preliminary work. These can be ideal places to start, and the peer feedback you receive can powerfully shape your ongoing work. At the same time, publishing or presenting papers in peer-reviewed venues like international journals and conferences can be a motivating intellectual challenge and an effective way to join larger SoTL conversations. Many of us, in fact, may need such peer-reviewed publications for job applications, promotion, tenure, or other career reasons, and that's not a bad thing.

If you worry about scholarly "double-dipping" (i.e., presenting the same thing in different places), you can think carefully about what you share where and how to craft different portions of your work for different audiences. We've found that even the seemingly simplest or smallest SoTL inquiries can generate multiple possibilities, such as the following:

- A focused reporting on the project itself (i.e., what you did, how you did it and why, and what you learned)
- A reflective piece on what you learned about yourself through the SoTL inquiry process
- A critical analysis of a conceptual framework or the method you used, and its promise for others' SoTL inquiries
- A review of the literature on your topic

And there are probably more. In table 10.1, we've compile recommendations and accompanying resources for sharing your SoTL.

Table 10.1. Recommendations and resources for sharing your SoTL

Recommendation	Supporting Resources and Examples
Start by recognizing the common ground between your disciplinary ways of sharing your work and those used in SoTL. To ease your transition into SoTL, you might first go public in ways that are familiar to you already.	"Reconciling Apples & Oranges: A Constructivist SoTL Writing Program" by Nancy L. Chick, La Vonne Cornell-Swanson, Katina Lazarides, and Renee Meyers (2014)
Reflect on the story you'll be telling as you share your SoTL. *Hint:* it doesn't have to be a success story, and it doesn't have to fit into a narrow set of academic writing forms.	"The Morphology of the SoTL Article: New Possibilities for the Stories That SoTL Scholars Tell About Teaching and Learning" by Faye Halpern (2023) "Making Space for Failure in the Scholarship of Teaching and Learning: A Blueprint" by Nancy L. Chick, Laura Cruz, Jennifer C. Friberg, and Hillary H. Steiner (2023) "Reading the Stories of Teaching and Learning" by Karen Manarin (2017)
Include your own experiences and reflections when you share your SoTL.	"Scholarly Personal Narrative in the SoTL Tent" by Laura Ng and Mary A. Carney (2017)

	"The First Person" by Helen Sword (2019)

"Great Introspections: How and Why SoTL Looks Inward" by Gary Poole and Nancy Chick (2022)

"Legitimizing Reflective Writing in SoTL" by Alison Cook-Sather, Sophia Abbot, and Peter Felten (2019) |
| As you think about your word choices and style, attend to the diversity of SoTL readers and audiences. | "Writing for Diverse Audiences" guide from *Teaching & Learning Inquiry*

"Internationalising a Journal Article" by Pat Thomson (2017) |
| Explore some nuts-and-bolts guidance on how to craft some of the genres in SoTL, including more traditional academic genres like empirical research articles, case studies, book chapters, and poster presentations to more public venues like social media, blogs, and mainstream media. | *Writing About Learning and Teaching in Higher Education: Creating and Contributing to Scholarly Conversations across a Range of Genres* by Mick Healey, Kelly Matthews, and Alison Cook-Sather (2020)

"Posters: Visual Representations of SoTL Projects" by Nancy L. Chick (2025)

"Social Media and Public SoTL" by Jessie Moore, Claire Hamshire, and Peter Felten (2022) |

	"Making Scholarship of Teaching and Learning Public Using Weblogs" by Jennifer C. Friberg, Lauren Scharff, John Draeger, and Aaron S. Richmond (2022) "The Scholarship of Teaching and Learning and Traditional Media" by Lee Skallerup Bessette (2022)
Think carefully about who you are (and who you aren't citing) and use your work to lift up scholars and voices that you believe merit additional presence in SoTL conversations.	"Who Are We Citing and How? A SoTL Citation Analysis" by Alicia Cappello and Janice Miller-Young (2020) "Naming Is Power: Citation Practices in SoTL" by Nancy L. Chick, Sophia Abbot, Lucy Mercer-Mapstone, Christopher P. Ostrowdun, and Krista Grensavitch (2021) "Can SoTL Generate High Quality Research while Maintaining its Commitment to Inclusivity?" by Jill McSweeney and Matthew A. Schnurr (2023)

Peer Review in SoTL

Peer review is one of the fundamental drivers of quality in most forms of scholarship. Norwegian professor of education Gunnar Handal (1999) points to its role also as a driver of new knowledge: "Without criticism of existing knowledge we would experience almost no scientific progress" (59). In the history of SoTL, key scholars also have emphasized how peer review is an essential part of what makes this kind of inquiry a form of "scholarship." Following Ernest Boyer's death, three of his colleagues at the Carnegie Foundation—Charles E. Glassick, Mary Taylor Huber, and Gene I. Maeroff—extended his argument from *Scholarship Reconsidered: Priorities of the Professoriate* (1990) into their book *Scholarship Assessed: Evaluation of the Professoriate* (1997). In this book, the authors list six criteria for scholarship, including "effective presentation…to reach the intended audience" and "reflective critique" by oneself and others as components of all scholarly activity (31–35).

As academics, we experience peer review acutely when we apply for an academic position or promotion, propose a conference session, or submit a manuscript to a journal. We also find it in research seminars and in PhD defenses, and sometimes in department meetings and even email exchanges. These experiences can be exhilarating when we receive affirming or constructively challenging feedback that makes us feel like full and valued members of a scholarly community. At other times, these experiences can be deflating, sparking doubts about our capacities as a scholar and our place in the academy (as the Facebook group "Reviewer 2 must be stopped" and "Reviewer 2" memes showcase).

Peer review, then, is an essential part of SoTL, but not just any form of peer review will do. Your disciplinary norms of peer review may or may not translate into what you experience in SoTL. Michael Anthony Samuel (2017) says that the "general scrutiny" of disciplinary peer review often devolves into "the promotion of self-indulgent rhetoric," but SoTL peer review should be "about actively putting one's ideas up for challenge to seek new alternatives" and different perspectives that serve "conscious decision-making" (26). Indeed, we have often experienced an ethos of peer review that reflects SoTL's diverse, multidisciplinary, and generous SoTL community. To be sure, reviews that sound like Reviewer 2 or Samuel's self-indulgent rhetoricians occasionally pop up, but they are far fewer in SoTL. As authors, former journal editors, and members of the SoTL community, we often find—and advocate for—an intentional orientation toward collegial, developmental, and supportive peer review, a spirit captured in Nancy's (2024) article, "'Dear Author': A Transparent SoTL Peer Review."

This approach is also embraced, promoted, and rewarded by the International Society for the Scholarship of Teaching and Learning (ISSOTL), the field's professional organization. This ethos, which Sarah Bunnell and Susannah McGowan (2024) call "the ceremony of SoTL welcome" (41), is shared with those who attend its annual conference through the ISSOTL Conference Pedagogy, which stresses that "our presentation styles—regardless of session type—encourage conversation, facilitate interaction (or even active learning), solicit feedback, and of course invite questions," and "We listen across differences, asking what we can learn from others about our own situations. We ask questions that call for answers by multiple scholars from a variety of cultural and disciplinary contexts" (Chick, Bunnell, Felten, Higgs, Long, Manarin, Marquis, Mårtensson, Matthews, Moore, and Scharff 2017) Also, the instructions for peer reviewers of ISSOTL's journal, *Teaching & Learning Inquiry*, stipulate that reviewers should hold high standards while "providing constructive criticism in a professional and collegial manner" and encourage "reviewers to approach the process with a mentoring mindset" (*Teaching & Learning Inquiry*, n.d.) And to further promote and celebrate this developmental approach to peer review, the journal also grants an annual [Gary Poole Distinguished Reviewer Award](), in honor of the ways in which one of its founding coeditors embraced and enacted that spirit, along with the expectation of systematic approaches and meaningful contributions in SoTL inquiries.

In the end, we encourage you to situate your thinking about peer review in SoTL within this chapter and others in this book. Think of it as part of the process of entering an ongoing conversation. Yes, everyone in this particular conversation may be blindfolded, but your goal in joining them is to invite these conversation partners to care enough to push and prod in ways that make your SoTL work, and you, stronger. We began this book with an emphasis on the people—our (Nancy, Peter, and Katarina) relationships with each other and other colleagues, and you as you bring your whole self to your work and to this work. In the final section of this book, we'll delve into some other ways engaging in SoTL may affect you as an individual ([chapter 11]()) and as part of a community of scholars ([chapter 12]()).

Questions for You

We invite you to explore these questions in individual reflection or collegial conversation:

- Reflect on the 6 Ps outlined in this chapter (i.e., *pragmatic, policy, professional, purpose, participation,* and *public*). What do they help you notice about your SoTL practice?

- What are your most significant experiences with scholarly peer review? How might SoTL's orientation toward collegial, developmental, and supportive peer review support or challenge you?
- What are one or two ways you could extend your SoTL work even further into the public?

Supplemental Materials

- Table: Recommendations and Resources for Sharing Your SoTL
- Video: Four SoTL luminaries describe a variety of ways to think about going public with SoTL in this video (7:31) produced by the Center for Engaged Learning.

SECTION 3

Looking Ahead

CHAPTER 11

For You as an Individual

In this final section, we shift our attention from developing your SoTL project to focusing on the implications of doing SoTL. Of course, as we've shared throughout this book, a significant implication of your SoTL practice is how it ultimately supports students' learning (Trigwell 2013), and depending on the questions you explore, SoTL can have "implications not just for students' academic learning and personal flourishing but also for creating greater social justice in the world" (Kreber 2013, 11). But just as we began this book by inviting you to think about how engaging in SoTL can matter and be meaningful to you, we want to return to you in our final section—first, for you as an individual (this chapter) and then, for you in a community of scholars ([chapter 12](#)).

These two topics are not always distinct. The individual and communal consequences of your SoTL project might be intertwined if you're developing a SoTL inquiry within a program, institution, or discipline that supports this work. If you're on your own in your SoTL ventures, however, you might be more likely to first see the individual effects before you find yourself in a community (or communities) of like-minded scholars.

In chapter 2, before you started designing your SoTL project, we encouraged you to think about how *who you are shapes what you do*. Now that you've done (or planned) at least one SoTL project, we'll invert that thought and invite you to consider how *what you do shapes who you are* (figure 11.1). We'll begin by considering how engaging in SoTL may affect *what you do* as an individual, particularly in your teaching and in your scholarly activities. We'll conclude the chapter by reflecting on how SoTL may influence *who you are*, or how you understand your professional identity.

> **Who you are shapes what you do**
> **What you do shapes who you are**

Figure 11.1. Ambigram of "Who you are shapes what you do." / "What you do shapes who you are."

These implications of SoTL engagement may be completely new to you, leading to dramatic changes, or they may simply amplify what you already do, feel, or know. As some of our examples in this chapter suggest, many longtime SoTL practitioners continue to be transformed by this work, even after many projects or years. We certainly do.

We also recognize that the individual changes SoTL sparks may not always be—or feel—pleasant, at least not while they are happening. For instance, your first foray into SoTL, or your initial exploration of a new-to-you methodology or body of literature, may remind you of what you don't know. You may have encountered similar feelings as you gained expertise in your discipline. The scholar Anna Parkman (2016) has found that this "imposter phenomenon" is rampant in higher education, including among academic teachers. Feeling that way does not mean something is wrong with you or that SoTL is not right for you. Rather, impostorism is a common experience, and one that can be worked through with patience and persistence. Give yourself grace, and connect with colleagues. SoTL offers the potential for significant individual and community growth.

What You Do

Let's begin with what you do. Not what you do according to your job title or even your list of responsibilities, but what you do as part of your everyday academic life. What and how you prepare for your classes, how you show up in the classroom, how you think about your students, where you turn your scholarly lens, what questions interest you—all of these are actions shaped by your values, your commitments, and your ways of making sense of teaching and learning. Doing SoTL doesn't just inform these actions. It can shift them, gradually or dramatically. In the next sections, we'll explore some fo the most common ways SoTL practioners notice that their practice changes over time.

How You Teach

Teaching is where many of us feel the effects of SoTL most. The new perspectives we gain often show up first—and most clearly—in our classrooms. Sometimes the changes are subtle: a new way of framing a topic, a tweak to an assignment, a more intentional way of checking in with students. Other times, the changes are more sweeping, like rethinking a course structure or letting go of familiar practices that no longer align with what we've come to understand about learning. Below, we'll consider some of the specific implications on how you teach.

Implication 1: Becoming More Knowledgeable

First and foremost, doing SoTL will affect how you teach. Over time, you'll become a more knowledgeable teacher as you learn more. You may develop or hone a foundational conception of how teaching and learning work, and this approach will start to—or more frequently and intentionally—guide your teaching practices. You'll realize that what may seem like good teaching doesn't necessarily lead to student learning because, for example, what students know before they take your class has a powerful effect on their ability to integrate what you're teaching with their prior knowledge (Lovett, Bridges, DiPietro, Ambrose, and Norman 2023; National Academies 2018). You'll recognize how and why some teaching practices are more effective than others, and how some even inhibit your students' learning. You'll also see how this effectiveness is tied to whom, where, and when you teach, helping you become a more reflective and equity-minded teacher (Adams, Bell, Goodman, Shlasko, Briggs, and Pacheco 2022; Artze-Vega, Darby, Dewsbury, and Imad 2023; Brookfield 2017; Kumar and Refaei 2021). All of this knowledge will prompt you—over time—to revise your syllabi, redesign your courses, and develop new assignments and in-class activities to align with what you're learning. And we're not just saying that. Keith Trigwell (2013), who has studied this process through his career, concludes that "the teachers who adopt scholarly, inquiring, reflecting, peer reviewing, student-centred approaches to teaching are likely to be achieving the purpose of improving student learning" (102).

Lendol Calder, a historian at a liberal arts college in the US, is a good example of becoming a more knowledgeable teacher as he's engaged with SoTL over the years. When he began to inquire into student learning, he was disturbed to realize that the way historians teach "the typical, coverage-oriented survey" course so common in his discipline "must share in the blame for Americans' deplorable ignorance of history" (Calder 2006, 1359–1362). Inspired to change this, he redesigned his course to address students' misconceptions about history and to practice the ways of thinking that will prepare them "to do what historically minded people do" (1364). Fifteen years later, Calder is still growing as a teacher and implementing what he's learning in his classes. He and Robert Williams chip away at another cornerstone of traditional history courses by asking, "Might it be possible for students to learn historical thinking without having to write traditional college essays?" (Calder and Williams 2021, 10). Their SoTL project in two sections of a history survey, with only one section writing the typical five essays and both completing regular assessments of key moves in historical thinking, revealed two important lessons. First, they found virtually no difference between the two groups' historical skills at the end of the semester and, in fact, "that essay writing can sometimes depress historical thinking" (Calder and Williams 2021, 15). One small exception was "the *B* students" who were already proficient at analyzing the sources of historical documents: writing essays "seems to nudge them to higher levels of performance" in this specific skill but "did not appear to help other students learn how to source," a powerful finding about what works—and doesn't work—for whom (13–14). Ultimately, Calder and Williams admit that the enormous amount of work for students who write the essays and the teachers who grade them doesn't result in greater learning for the vast majority of students. Calder is just one example of how engaging in SoTL is, in some ways, about the practitioner's learning just as much as it is about students' learning.

Implication 2: Becoming More Confident Yet Humble

This ongoing learning will also make you a more confident yet humble teacher. As you do your own SoTL projects, and as you explore and learn more, you'll feel at once *more* confident in your teaching and *less* confident in your teaching, in part because you may be less confident in your effect on your students' learning. This paradox makes sense, though: as you gain insight into what you're doing well and integrate even more effective practices, you'll also surface plenty of aspects of your teaching that don't achieve what you hoped for, for a variety of reasons. You'll also become more aware of what you don't know, as typically happens with increasing knowledge. As you see the breadth of existing research and scholarship on teaching and learning in higher education, you'll want to read more. But you can't read everything, and even if you did have time, the different bodies of research that can inform your teaching practice are diverse and dispersed across fields. You'll want to change parts of how you teach, but change can take time, so you do what you can. As survey respondents explained in a study of faculty learning processes through SoTL, the more you learn, the more "'comfortable'" you'll become "'in trying new things even if they [are] not 'perfect' the first go around" and in "'evaluating them from a variety of perspectives to keep [your] teaching dynamic'" (Gayle,

Randall, Langley, and Preiss 2013, 88). You may find this courage to experiment and rethink your long-held beliefs about teaching.

All of this critical self-evaluation can be hard for academics, who often are grounded in their sense of expertise. For the majority of us, our primary expertise is in our home disciplines, and SoTL is something we come to later, or as a secondary interest. Comparing how much we know about teaching and learning, then, with how much we know about our disciplinary expertise can lead to feelings of being an "amateur," an identity that's at odds with our typical self-image of expert (Pace 2004, 1171). Because of these realities, SoTL tends to keep us humble. Staying grounded in the reasons you're doing SoTL (chapter 2) can help you navigate these emotional challenges about teaching and identity (Boyd 2024).

Implication 3: Becoming More Empathetic

Doing SoTL will also make you a more empathetic teacher. You'll learn a lot about the students in your own classes and students elsewhere. You'll think less about the generic, decontextualized, or idealized student and more about the specific students you teach—the individual students, specific groups of students, and the differences between students even within the same group or class. This kind of empathy will also make you even more equitable in your teaching practices. You'll see more of who your students are and better understand why they excel in some areas and struggle in others, and why they prefer some things and resist others. You'll become even more aware of how your students are multifaceted humans with lives well beyond your classroom, and how they bring a wealth of knowledge and experiences to what and how they learn. You'll also recognize how often you're wrong in your assumptions about your students.

Dianne Fallon (2006) illustrates this shift in thinking as a result of a SoTL project she conducted on her students' unexpected responses to racial issues in her humanities course at a community college in a predominantly white state in the US. She writes, "Instead of feeling frustrated by what seemed to be, in some students, a regression or stasis in their understanding of diversity issues, I could look at these student comments, and others, as a source of data, as a place to begin developing *a richer understanding of how my students process and respond to diversity issues*" (emphasis added; 411). She then revised her inquiry, shifting away from her original plan of focusing on a single assignment to understanding her students' responses more broadly. In doing so, she learned that her students' thinking was complex and recursive, "not a linear process but instead characterized by fits and starts" as they wrestled with difficult issues (415). In the end, she described SoTL's "common focus on trying to understand student responses to diversity issues rather than… characterizing the students as problematic" (416). This shift away from blaming students for the expected messiness of learning processes is profound.

Implication 4: Becoming More Transparent

You'll also become more transparent in your teaching as you share what you're learning with your students. As doing SoTL helps you think carefully through your teaching practice, you'll explain your intentional choices in course and assignment design, class activity structure, text selection, and more. You'll also be explicit about these choices because you know that such transparency "promot[es] students' conscious understanding of how they learn," which "reduce[s] systemic inequities in higher education" (Winkelmes 2023). You may even go meta by being transparent about your transparency as you share your own experiences in learning through SoTL. Giving students a glimpse behind the curtain of your teaching practice may feel vulnerable, but this transparency helps them understand the often invisible codes and customs (or the "hidden curriculum") of higher education and models how experts continue to learn and reflect throughout their career. Even further, Trent Maurer, Cherie Woolmer, Nichole Powell, Carol Sisson, Catherine Snelling, Odd Rune Stalheim, and Ian Turner (2021), SoTL scholars from Australia, Canada, Norway, the UK, and the US, argue that sharing with students what you learn through SoTL inquiries is caring, disrupts traditional power structures, enacts a reflective teaching practice, and improves the quality of the scholarship itself.

How You Do Scholarly Activities

While the influence of SoTL on teaching may seem most obvious, it also has a way of expanding our understanding of scholarship itself. For many, a single project can spark a shift in how they think about their scholarly work—what questions they pursue, what counts as meaningful inquiry, and how their research can contribute to teaching and learning. SoTL can reshape your scholarly trajectory, widen your intellectual networks, and offer a new kind of scholarly home. In the following sections, we'll consider how doing SoTL may lead you to pursue new lines of inquiry, engage more fully with the broader field, or even reimagine your scholarly identity.

Implication 5: Pursuing More SoTL Projects

In addition to informing your teaching, doing SoTL may also influence your scholarly interests and activities. Before now, your scholarly activities—whether you think about these activities as scholarship, research, or creative expression—may have been focused on your disciplinary subject matter or a prior research agenda. You may now find that your experience with SoTL expands how you think about this part of your work, and you may even decide to go beyond a single project and stay engaged in SoTL in some sustained way, making SoTL one aspect of your scholarly activity or maybe even beginning to center SoTL in your scholarship (Miller-Young and Chick 2024).

Perhaps, for example, you'll find that SoTL questions and project ideas bubble up as part of your regular professional activities. Something that happens in a class or in a conversation with students will inspire you, or an idea from a reading will raise interesting questions within your specific context, or your current SoTL inquiry may lead to a follow-up project. Many SoTL practitioners find that, after they get started, they see SoTL opportunities all around. This orientation, combined with your growing knowledge, may lead you toward a specific area of SoTL inquiry. Some even more fully integrate SoTL into their work and, over time, end up with what looks like a SoTL research agenda. (Some are genuine research agendas mapped out intentionally, and others just unfold as their areas of interest build on each other.)

Sherry Linkon, for example, started out with a SoTL project to understand why interdisciplinary thinking was so challenging for her students, who largely majored in single disciplines at a university in the US. She explains that the "real vision-changing experience" for her was the SoTL task of analyzing student work when she first "sat down and looked closely at a piece of student writing as a 'window' on the learning process" (Linkon 2000, 64). Linkon has remained an active scholar in her discipline of literary studies and the interdisciplinary field of working-class studies, but she also has continued to explore these themes from her first SoTL project. To name just a few products of that exploration, she and Randy Bass wrote an article arguing for more close reading of student writing as artifacts of learning in SoTL (Bass and Linkon 2008), she and Stephen Bloch-Schulman coedited a special issue of *Teaching & Learning Inquiry* focused on SoTL in the arts and humanities (2016), and she published *Literary Learning: Teaching the English Major* as part of Indiana University Press's SoTL book series (2011).

Implication 6: Going Further Afield with SoTL

You may also decide to engage in the broader field of SoTL. Your initial project may have piqued your curiosity about what you can learn by becoming a student of SoTL, so you fold SoTL publications, conferences, social media, webinars, or podcasts into your professional routines. You may start keeping up with the pedagogy journals in your discipline or some multidisciplinary SoTL journals by bookmarking their websites or signing up for their content alert emails. Perhaps you'll wonder about others' inquiries in your discipline or topic area, your type of institution, or your geographical and cultural context.

You may even reach farther outside of the issues that seem immediately relevant to you. Some SoTL practitioners point to this curiosity as a reminder of why they got involved with higher education in the first place: the joy of learning. Peter, for example, keeps up with—and occasionally contributes to—a range of social media accounts related to SoTL, educational development, and higher education, connecting him to scholarship and scholars from around the world (for more on social media and SoTL, see Moore, Hamshire, and Felten 2022). Nancy regularly reads *CBE—Life Sciences Education* (a journal published by the American Society for Cell Biology) and *Teaching English in the Two-Year College* (a disciplinary journal focused on a specific kind of institution) because of the quality of their articles and what she learns from them, even though the first isn't related to her home discipline (literary studies) and the other to her institutional context. Katarina browses broadly across social media, podcasts, newsletters, and journals in the field of higher education as a way to stimulate the joy of learning. Each of us also takes many opportunities to engage in conversations with colleagues locally and internationally because they always give food for thought.

Who You Are

All of the above are some possible ways in which engaging in SoTL may influence what you do as a teacher and a scholar. Since what you do can shape who you are, there's a good chance that engaging in SoTL also will have some effect on your professional identity, or how you think about who you are. Your SoTL activities and your SoTL-informed teaching practice will likely affect how you think about yourself *as a teacher*. Given the above transformations, you may see yourself as a more knowledgeable, a more confident yet humble, a more empathetic, and/or a more transparent teacher. Any one of these is a good thing. More than one of these transformations is even better. These shifts in how you think about yourself can deepen your sense of purpose or commitment, both of which contribute to feelings of agency and professional growth (O'Meara, LaPointe Terosky, and Neumann 2008) and mitigate burnout (Pope-Ruark 2022).

Implication 7: Seeing Yourself as a Teacher

You may also be thinking more about yourself as a teacher as part of *who you are* and not just *what you do*. Not all academics embrace—or are trained to think of—*teacher* as part of their professional identity. For many of us, our disciplinary and scholarly identity predates our introduction to SoTL, although there's evidence that a new generation of SoTL scholars may be emerging as some begin their careers—even their schooling—within SoTL (Bunnell, Chick, Hamilton, Santucci Leoni, and Woolmer 2024). But if you're coming from traditional academic training grounded in a discipline, your disciplinary identity will probably remain foremost in your thoughts as you engage with SoTL (Mårtensson, Roxå, and Olsson 2011). In this case, any new identity might challenge this deeply rooted sense of who you are professionally because "when people's identities are at stake, passions run deep" (Becher and Trowler 2001, 126).

In fact, Sara E. Brownell and Kimberly D. Tanner (2012), biologists in the US, write about this resistance grounded in strong disciplinary identities. Although their work focuses on scientists, much of the tension they describe could be applied (perhaps with less intensity) to many other disciplines. They note how most academic training cultivates the specific identity of "researcher," sometimes explicitly to the exclusion of "teacher," so even those who embrace a teaching identity may be "afraid to 'come out' as teachers" to their peers (Brownell and Tanner 2012, 341). A similar dynamic exists in professional fields, too, where academics are often trained to think of themselves primarily as clinicians or researchers, not educators (Stenfors-Hayes, Weurlander, Dahlgren, and Hult 2010).

Implication 8: Seeing Yourself as a SoTL Practitioner

This ambivalence about the identity of *teacher* could also be said about *SoTL practitioner* or *SoTL scholar*, which might even feel more at odds with your identity as a disciplinary scholar or researcher. Even if the differences are subtle, such as within those disciplines that have long centered research on their students' learning, your disciplinary identity may be so deeply embedded in who you are that any distinctions will likely surface at some point.

In their 2013 article exploring identity in SoTL, Nicola Simmons, Earle Abrahamson, Jessica M. Deshler, Barbara Kensington-Miller, Karen Manarin, Sue Morón-García, Carolyn Oliver, and Joanna Renc-Roe (SoTL scholars from different countries, disciplines, and career stages) describe some internal conflicts as they observe differences between their disciplinary work and SoTL. In analyzing each other's narratives about their SoTL experiences, they see moments of "self-questioning, discomfort, and risk taking," elements of "an ongoing identity struggle" as the traction of their disciplinary work resists integrating their SoTL work (13). Sophia Abbot, who first entered SoTL as an undergraduate student partner in SoTL inquiries in the US, articulates a question probably asked by "Each person entering SoTL": "How does SoTL fit into the research story one was hired to tell?" (2024, 39–40) Reflecting on this same issue, Nattalia Godbold, Dawne Irving-Bell, Jill McSweeney-Flaherty, Patrice Torcivia, Lauren Schlesselman, and Heather Smith (2021), another group diverse in location, discipline, and career stage, emphasize the "courage" necessary to engage in the often-liminal work of SoTL.

It may also be hard to think of yourself as either a *teacher* or a *SoTL practitioner* or *scholar* if you're at an institution that elevates the status of research over teaching. Recall that this kind of institutional culture and the resulting undervaluing of the work academics do as teachers are foundational to Boyer's (1990) argument for expanding "the work of the professoriate" to include the scholarship of teaching and learning. If you are not in a context that embraces—or perhaps even allows for—SoTL, then you might see your engagement with this work and community as either an act of resistance or a way to open up a nurturing "third space" professionally (McIntosh and Nutt 2022).

In *Becoming a SoTL Scholar,* Janice Miller-Young and Nancy Chick (2024) explain that their title acknowledges the complexity of "reckoning with one's academic identity" and that all identity formation is ongoing, so "one is always ... becoming" (6). Indeed, Simmons, Deshler, Kensington-Miller, Manarin, Morón-García, Oliver, and Renc-Roe (2013) note that most of us will always be negotiating and renegotiating the relationship between our disciplinary and SoTL work—and thus between our disciplinary selves and our SoTL selves. Even though they present their analyses simply as themes and not stages, they describe a moment of "crossing an identity threshold" with the emergence of a SoTL identity (2013, 14). Often prompted by some epiphany about SoTL, this "SoTL self-construction" relieves some of that internal conflict by imagining "a new way of being an academic" (2013, 14). In an article by Bunnell, Chick, Hamilton, Santucci Leoni, and Woolmer (2024), Cherie Woolmer describes herself as "nomadic" in terms of disciplines but gradually finding in

SoTL "a space to disrupt the idea of the scholar I thought was required in academia" and "a space for me to become a version of the academic that *celebrates* disciplinary breadth, commits to transformational education, and tries to disrupt hegemonic practices" (35). Abbot (2024) describes her path as a student seeking a career in SoTL, rather than a traditional discipline, so SoTL became "the space I burrowed for myself in academia," and she became what she calls "a SoTL citizen" (43).

Implication 9: Seeing Yourself as Belonging

Finally, in their exploration of SoTL identity, Simmons and her colleagues (2013) present a theme that (unlike the other themes they observed) was common to all eight of them. Each of their SoTL narratives include finding "a sense of belonging" and even "a second home" in SoTL, often as they collaborate with other SoTL colleagues (15–16). This theme speaks to the sense of community many find when they engage in SoTL, perhaps the most transformational aspect of engaging with SoTL.

Of course, many academics engaged in SoTL do not experience a professional transformation; instead, SoTL is something they do without being fully part of who they are professionally. Yet by doing SoTL they—both you and we—are joining and contributing to an ongoing scholarly conversation about teaching and learning. Everyone's voice belongs in that conversation, no matter if you're a SoTL traveler or citizen (Abbot 2024).

This sense of ourselves as working within a community of scholars who share the same interests and passions, regardless of discipline, geographical location, and even culture, is the topic of the next and final chapter.

Questions for You

We invite you to explore these questions in individual reflection or collegial conversation:
- What are your hopes and plans for how SoTL influences your work and your career?
- Do any of the implications described above inspire or challenge you? Why?
- In what ways do you feel you belong in SoTL? What ways would you like to belong?

Supplemental Materials

Worksheet: Reflecting on SoTL and You

CHAPTER 12

For You in a Community of Scholars

We will close this book by reflecting on why Burke's metaphor for scholarly conversations resonates for us and for so many academics. The idea of entering a room where lots of people are talking to each other and then joining their conversations is familiar because we're all part of the knowledge and discourse communities of our home disciplines. This disciplinary room (or rooms) is what many of us think of as our community of scholars (or researchers, or artists, scientists, artists, engineers, etc.). Some may also think about their campuses or perhaps their online scholarly spaces as their community: it's where they spend most of their time, interact with colleagues, and often commit to a decades-long relationship.

So why are we ending *The SoTL Guide* with a chapter about you in a community of scholars, as if you aren't already? We want to leave you with an invitation to expand how you think about your community. We have come to consider SoTL not just something we do (or have done) but also one of our communities, one that has inspired and sustained us over the years. Also, our experiences of being in this community have changed how we understand the meaning of *community*. We're not suggesting that you would want to leave or contribute any less to your disciplinary, institutional, or any other current community, or that you need to immerse yourself in SoTL as the focus of your work. Sophia Abbot's (2024) observation that "there are more travelers in SoTL than there are citizens" (39) captures how, for many, engagement in SoTL waxes and wanes over time (as does how they think about their community or communities) depending on their situation, context, goals, interests, and capacities.

We also want to explain how we're using the word *community*. We're not simply talking about a collection of people who are loosely held together by circumstance, like those who live in the same neighborhood. Instead, we're talking about a group of people who share a deep engagement in a certain practice (like teaching) and who are committed to doing that as best as they can and to continue developing themselves and that practice. They don't necessarily do things in the same way, nor do they necessarily belong to the same context—on the contrary, in fact, as you've seen throughout this book with our emphasis on differing contexts. The richness of this kind of community is the shared engagement in something that centers our attention and efforts. In the case of SoTL, the shared engagement is the care for students' experiences and learning, and the commitment to developing teaching and knowledge about teaching for that purpose. The community members' sense of common purpose (broad or specific) and some degree of a collective identity and relationship also matter. And while the general definition of *community of practice*—"groups of people who share a concern or passion for something they do and learn how to do it better as they interact regularly" (Wenger-Trayner and Wenger-Trayner 2015)—is helpful, that specific term comes with a body of literature that's more precise and bounded than we intend.

We also refer to *community* as both a count and noncount noun. On one hand, we all belong to multiple communities we can count: a discipline, a campus, and more. On the other hand, we also experience an uncountable *sense of* community, a feeling of being part of something, of belonging. Finally, we also think about *community* as more than a noun, or a thing that exists. It's also a practice, a process, or even a praxis—an honorary verb, if you will.

To illustrate, we often hear new-to-SoTL colleagues echo Michelle Eady's (2024) observations about what happens when we first meet others doing SoTL. A scholar in Australia, Eady reflects on her personal experiences with the moment of first meeting other SoTL practitioners at a conference: "Finding such connections and developing a sense of community with SoTL colleagues can feel like coming home to a familiar, caring, and intellectual group of scholars who also want to be that difference in higher education" (256). In this brief quote, she captures all of our intended meanings of *community*:

- Finding a new "group of" colleagues "who also want" to work toward a common purpose (a new-to-her community as a group of people with a shared commitment)
- Feeling "like coming home" (a sense of community as being warmly welcomed, connected, and at ease)
- Actively "developing" or contributing to the group's experience (community as a practice)

There's something else worth pointing out in Eady's quote. Implied in her description of "finding such connections" is an openness to something new, as in Abbot's (2024) metaphor of SoTL "travelers filled with the possibility of transformation" (37). Both phrases speak to being receptive to the unexpected. SoTL often reveals the unexpected about students' learning, can present unanticipated opportunities to connect with colleagues and purposes in ways that make our professional work more meaningful.

Expanding Your Communities

There are lots of reasons why you may decide to reach beyond your existing communities of your discipline or institution. You may be interested in a new community if your campus—or your virtual workplace—feels divided into the small, insulated, and even claustrophobic communities behind the ubiquitous academic metaphor of *silos*. Perhaps you're simply eager to find colleagues who share your new interest in SoTL, or your long-held passions and commitments. Or maybe you find the existing spaces of your discipline or institution unfulfilling, chilly, or so familiar that they no longer inspire you. Or perhaps you're experiencing the mid-career doldrums of having achieved significant academic goals, such as tenure, promotion, a strong record of publication, excellent teaching reviews, or some other successes, and you're now looking for something new and different to reenergize yourself. For some of you, it may be as simple as looking for a place to grow. These are just some of the conditions that have nudged others to seek out or stumble upon a new community of scholars through their engagement with SoTL.

"The SoTL Community"

You may hear or read about *the SoTL community* (including in this book), suggesting a single, all-encompassing community. While on some level this idea oversimplifies a highly diverse and diffuse group, it's still meaningful. The notion of a SoTL community owes its origin to Boyer. As we mentioned in chapter 1, although some disciplines had long been doing some variation of inquiry into students' learning, Boyer coined the term "the scholarship of teaching" in his 1990 book. This textual moment is significant for lots of reasons, including its role in creating the epistemic space for academics from any discipline to come together in a "self-aware, intentional" community committed to teaching (Chick 2018, 7). This community quickly became international, as well, even though the term *the scholarship of teaching and learning* doesn't easily translate into many languages, as we also described in chapter 1. You may recall that the translations subtly change the meaning of the term (box 1.1). What's important here is that people from all of these different languages are actually trying to translate it, suggesting that the umbrella term, while multilingually awkward, has brought people together from across these different contexts.

The sense of an overarching SoTL community was strengthened by the founding of an international professional organization for SoTL. Since 2004, the International Society for the Scholarship of Teaching and Learning (ISSOTL) has brought together academics whose common ground is an interest in doing, supporting, or promoting SoTL. This professionalization of SoTL includes membership dues, an annual conference, a peer-reviewed journal, interest groups, and more, all of which contribute to what many experience as *a SoTL community,* whether they are dues-paying members or they just know about the organization. Even further, some of ISSOTL's founders and subsequent officers are also authors of some of the post-Boyer foundational texts in SoTL, interlacing the organization and some of the major tenets of the field. All of these developments have deepened the sense of SoTL as both a knowledge and discourse community and a community of people with a shared interest.

"SoTL Communities"

At the same time, there isn't just one SoTL community. Even within ISSOTL, members of some of the interest groups or specific world regions within ISSOTL may consider these focused groups their primary SoTL community, which happens to be supported by the infrastructure of the larger organization. One of the great truths about those who engage in SoTL is their diversity. We've touched on some of the differences (e.g., discipline, institution type, career stage, nationality, language), but there's also variety in how and how much they engage in SoTL. Specifically, not everyone interested in SoTL thinks about an overarching SoTL community, much less considers themselves part of it, and for plenty of reasons. You may, for example, prefer organizations within your specific region (e.g., EuroSoTL for Europe, SoTL in the South for the global south, Latin SoTL for Latin America, China SoTL for China) or subject area (e.g., History SoTL). Or you may think about SoTL within the local context of the program or office where you learned about it or developed your project. And of course some of you may prefer the more organic communities of the people you meet, like, and want to stay in touch with.

And of course, all of the above can be true: there is a SoTL community, as well as many SoTL communities, and you can be part of as many or as few as you want.

Our SoTL Community

The three of us consider ourselves part of the SoTL community. We met at an ISSOTL conference and got to know each other through various roles in that organization, so in many ways we think of the international community under ISSOTL's umbrella as our community. But we also hold different types of positions in different types of institutions, come from different disciplines, are located on two separate continents with different languages, and have SoTL-related passions and interests that we may appreciate but don't necessarily hold in common. We may even name other SoTL communities that are equally but differently important to us at any particular moment in time. For example, Katarina thinks of the people who attend the biannual EuroSoTL conference as one of her SoTL communities.

A Diverse and Collaborative Community

SoTL also invites you to expand who you include as part of that community. We occasionally hear someone new to SoTL say, "I found my people." Our impression is that a statement like this isn't meant to be cliquish but rather is an expression of joy and surprise at finding colleagues who share similar passions and trajectories, especially if they don't find such connections in their existing communities or contexts. This can be particularly rewarding because the entry into SoTL communities can be different from the entrance into other academic communities.

Most of the people you encounter in SoTL communities will be professional peers. Academics often ascribe to the strictest sense of the word: a peer is someone who's "equal to another in abilities, qualifications, age, background, and social status" (dictionary.com). We tend to first think of fellow academics who fall within the common routines or rhythms of academic life, especially our disciplinary colleagues who also share our advanced degrees, body of knowledge, and epistemological worldview. We often start in these academic communities as graduate students with perhaps little status or expertise, initiating a deep feeling of hierarchy that can remain even as we progress through a career. Also, some of our disciplinary colleagues might have significant power in our professional progression (e.g., on promotion committees, as manuscript or grant reviewers), so these relationships sometimes remain at arm's length. The breadth of and diversity within the SoTL community makes many of these hierarchies less relevant. That's not to say hierarchies don't exist in SoTL communities. However, since paths into SoTL are so varied, and since those paths usually don't involve the often rigid experiences of graduate training, the politics of departmental decision-making, or the evaluative moments of promotion, SoTL relationships are often (or have the potential to be) more collaborative, equal, and authentic.

Indeed, in SoTL, you'll meaningfully engage with others who come from outside of your department, your institution, and your discipline, minimizing the evaluative power dynamics that often govern academic life. You may realize this first in SoTL spaces like at a conference, in an event sponsored by your campus's center for teaching or faculty development, or even in reading outside of your usual venues. Eady (2024) writes about this epiphany at her first ISSOTL conference, which was my entry into the international SoTL community, and it changed my working life. I had been attending conferences for at least twenty years, but I had never experienced what it was like to enter a building with so many like-minded and enthusiastic scholars. I found myself bumping into people whose work I had read, and I saw researchers and practitioners who hail from Europe, Asia, Australia, North America, and South Africa come together for a common purpose to share, to learn, and to work together for the betterment of teaching and learning. (Eady 2024, 258)

As one of the authors in the self-study on SoTL identity, featured in our previous chapter, wrote in their anonymized narrative, *"thank goodness for SoTL colleagues in other disciplines"* (emphasis in original; Simmons, Deshler, Kensington-Miller, Manarin, Morón-García, Oliver, and Renc-Roe 2013, 15).

Collaboration is also widespread in the SoTL community and across SoTL communities, including across disciplines. This book is one example, and you've probably noticed this phenomenon throughout this book as we've cited many coauthored pieces, including some by large international collaborations. Even academics coming from disciplines where individual research is the norm (like Peter in history and Nancy in literary studies), co-inquiry and coauthorship can become both a source of inspiration—especially with people who bring different approaches and methods—and a productive and even joyful practice.

You may also notice students in these spaces, beyond the ones who SoTL practitioners are studying in their projects. An increasingly common practice in SoTL is what Peter named as the fourth of his five Principles of Good Practice in SoTL: "conducted in partnership with students" (2013, 123). As we've mentioned elsewhere in this book (e.g., box 1.3 in chapter 1, supplemental materials in chapter 6), the literature on "students as partners"—a term so ubiquitous that some call it a movement (Friberg 2016; Matthews 2019)—is vast, including *The International Journal for Students as Partners,* which is dedicated to partnership as both a topic and a practice.

Expanding Your Sense of Community

In addition to introducing you to new and different communities, engaging in SoTL may also expand your sense of community. Some SoTL practitioners have described coming to think about community *differently*. The exclamation "I found my people" is imbued with a second kind of surprise, namely a feeling they hadn't gotten from their existing communities. What's so unusual about this feeling, and what about SoTL communities engenders it?

Let's briefly return to Eady's (2024) description of "a familiar, caring, and intellectual group" (256). These new-to-her colleagues feel "familiar" not because they're similar to her typical colleagues but because it "feels like coming home to" them: they feel like family. They are welcoming and supportive, but there's also more than an emotional connection. Eady notes their intellect and that they "also want to be that difference in higher education," so there's both an overlap and exchange of knowledge and commitment (256). This experience is often at the heart of the give and take occurring in SoTL's "trading zone."

Katarina's ongoing research with her colleague Torgny Roxå gives us insight into such "sincere and serious" experiences of reciprocity (Roxå and Mårtensson 2009, 550). This work analyzes the characteristics and outcomes of what they call "significant conversations" among academic teachers. First, these moments are informal, private, typically occurring in "backstage" spaces where participants "behave in a more unrestricted way than when we are 'front stage'" (2009, 255). They're also permeated by feelings of trust that result from both mutual respect and a willingness to be vulnerable in talking about topics that seem "very personal," including "'problems, obstacles and challenges rising from the teaching practice; that is, 'real' difficulties" (2009, 552–553). These conversations are also "serious" and "intellectually intriguing" in that they're "not just small talk or a way to give and receive emotional support" but also are sites for reciprocal sense-making (2009, 553). Also, they're "significant" because participants "develop, or even sometimes drastically change, their personal understanding of teaching and learning" (2009, 548).

Conversations like these aren't commonplace in academia, and finding such conversation partners or "significant others" is challenging, especially in contexts that don't feel supportive (2009, 555). Such contexts are typically characterized by a lack of serious, engaging conversations about teaching, and even a lack of ambition to have such conversations. This may be due to many things, including sticking to old habits, prioritizing research over teaching, or even being too insecure to talk about one's very personal practice of teaching, as suggested by Shulman's (1993) notion of "pedagogical solitude" and Bass's (1999) point that it can feel shameful to admit to teaching "problems." But when local contexts encourage such conversations about teaching and learning, the size of one's significant network increases—doubles, in fact—and the character of the "microculture" potentially changes (Mårtensson and Roxå 2016, 554). These conversations also don't have to happen formally or in a structured way. Gabriela

Pleschová, Torgny Roxå, Kate Eileen Thomson, and Peter Felten (2021) describe the "conducive spaces" in which these conversations emerge. Confirming Roxå and Mårtensson's earlier work on these "backstage" settings, these spaces are "almost never … in formal university settings" and instead are in "liminal" spaces intentionally created by participants, ranging from writing groups and workshop breakouts to coffee shop meetups and Zoom happy hours (Pleschová, Roxå, Thomson, and Felten 2021, 206). This fact gives you some agency in initiating the conversations yourself with even just a few trusted colleagues, as illustrated by the campus change that began simply with conversations among a faculty member, a librarian, and an educational developer chronicled in "Reaching Across the Disciplines to Build a Grassroots SoTL Community" (Gillespie, Goodridge, and Hall 2024). By embracing a more expansive and inclusive sense of community, you open yourself up to finding new "significant others"—and to them finding you (Roxå and Mårtensson 2009).

Grounding Community in Purpose

SoTL communities are distinct because they are grounded in a particular set of purposes. Our definition of SoTL in chapter 1, echoing Boyer, describes *SoTL as inquiry into teaching and learning for the purposes of improving teaching and learning in context and contributing to what we know about teaching and learning, in support of the broader aims of higher education.* Within that definition, we see three purposes: improvement, connection, and contribution.

First, SoTL communities are rooted in individual and shared inquiry into learning and teaching in context, with the aim of improvement. That means we tend to assume a growth mindset about our work and our students. We could always grow as teachers, and students could always learn more deeply. A core purpose of SoTL is to make that happen. By doing that work in community, we break through the customary solitude of the classroom teacher. That's essential because teaching well is rewarding, yet also hard and sometimes frustrating work. Building a career of teaching well takes intention, persistence, and resilience. By approaching the challenging work of teaching—and teaching improvement—as a shared professional obligation and commitment, we multiply our capacity to succeed. And we also ensure the journey along the way will be more enjoyable and fulfilling.

Second, SoTL communities are rooted in human connections sustained by collegial conversations. Throughout this book, we typically frame these moments of connection as constructive, even transformative. That's appropriate, but we also know that talking about your teaching and your students' learning can make you feel vulnerable. Too often, having a teaching "problem" evokes shame (Bass 1999). Yet being brave enough to have these conversations actually strengthens SoTL communities. We build trust with colleagues and within communities through our willingness to listen generously to others and to speak honestly. These conversations nurture strong communities even as they also contribute to our shared knowledge of teaching and learning.

Third, SoTL communities aspire to make meaningful contributions through great teaching and effective learning; as Boyer wrote decades ago (using American higher education terminology):

> There is growing evidence that professors want, and need, better ways for the full range of their aspirations and commitments to be acknowledged. Faculty are expressing serious reservations about the enterprise to which they have committed their professional lives.

> This deeply rooted professional concern reflects, we believe, recognition that teaching is crucial, that integrative studies are increasingly consequential, and that, in addition to research, the work of the academy must relate to the world beyond the campus. (Boyer 1990, 117)

This shared ambition to make a difference in and beyond our classrooms—as relevant today as it was in 1990—is central to the aims and practices of SoTL. These purposes act as both a glue that binds SoTL communities together and a catalyst for continuing inquiries.

Doing Community

Finally, we encourage you to think about how you *do* community. You may have noticed in this chapter that SoTL communities can begin serendipitously, but then shift to intentional and active relationship-building. Those engaged in SoTL often begin with plans to do a project, not necessarily to find new colleagues or communities, but then something happens, often unexpectedly. Eady (2024) writes about "finding such connections," not "searching for such connections." She "found [herself] bumping into" authors she'd read, not "sought out" these authors. (The familiar phrase is "I found my people," not "I looked for my people.") These are chance experiences. What makes them memorable is what happens afterward.

In reflecting on her "SoTL Adventures (So Far)," Corinne A. Green (2024) describes getting involved "through somewhat serendipitous means" but then making "increasingly strategic and intentional moves" (52). Seven years later, she looks back and sees her path in SoTL as "planned serendipity, where I intentionally pursue certain opportunities while remaining open to others, not knowing exactly where they might lead" (54). Green's notion of planned serendipity is a common and helpful praxis in SoTL.

This chapter features Eady and Green in part because of an earlier collaboration they had with Marian McCarthy, Ashley B. Akenson, Briony Supple, Jacinta McKeon, and James G. R. Cronin (2020). Together, they coauthored an article about their shared disappointment in "leav[ing] the excitement and energy of [the 2016 ISSOTL conference] and return[ing] to our isolated offices in the corners of our institutions" (Green, Eady, McCarthy, Akenson, Supple, McKeon, and Cronin 2020, 44). After the conference, this group's response was to intentionally—even doggedly—stay in touch by forming an ongoing virtual group without a specific goal or product in mind, aside from maintaining this feeling of community they'd found at the conference. By the way, nine years later, all seven remain actively connected. Also, what you can't tell from just looking at the list of names is that this group was made up of a student, a retired university vice president, and full-time academics from Australia, the United States, and Ireland—a microcosm of the diversity of the larger SoTL community.

So you may *find* some fantastic colleagues and potential collaborators in SoTL, but for them to become a community, you'll need to nurture it. Being an observer or a lurker (to draw on social media language) who watches others interact, exchange, and build community may feel safe, but it doesn't give you many of the benefits of that community. To *be in community*, you need to *do* community by stepping away from the periphery and becoming an active participant.

This transition can feel risky, especially for academics who are used to "prestige" environments "where academic rigour and credibility are the main currencies"—and for those in roles and with identities that are marginalized in higher education (Pleschová, Torgny, Thomson, and Felten 2021, 201). Small steps can be helpful in this process of engagement, such as seeking out peers from other disciplines with similar interests (perhaps through your campus teaching center), or expressing generous curiosity through questions you ask of colleagues, or soliciting guidance on your own work from more established members of the community. You can also develop your trust and trustworthiness in this process by putting trust in others (Pleschová, Sutherland, Felten, Forsyth, and Wright 2025). As you begin to join conversations in this community, be a generous contributor who shares the space and who invites others into the mix. These steps build connectedness among and efficacy within those in the community, which makes the group more open and constructive in both the short- and long-term (Wenger 2000).

Community as a Way of Being in SoTL

Our understanding of community in this final chapter is interwoven with our thinking about SoTL throughout this book, such as orienting to

- SoTL as a way to pursuing your professional passions and commitments to something bigger
- SoTL as an entry point into a trading zone of scholarly give and take
- The SoTL literature review as an ongoing conversation
- SoTL's ethical considerations as cultivating relationships rooted in care and transparency
- SoTL data or evidence as artifacts as traces of complex human learning

- Going public in SoTL as building community based in scholarly inquiry and shared purposes

Ultimately, perhaps the main reason we three remain so immersed in SoTL is because of the field's commitment to honoring the human experience in and through our work.

We leave you with a characteristic of the field that, we hope, reinforces the invitational orientation of this book. Just as each of us "is always … becoming" (Miller-Young and Chick 2024, 6), so too is SoTL. Boyer's original articulation of a Scholarship of Teaching (1990) soon added "and Learning." Early SoTL tended to focus on "problems" (Bass 1999) that individual academic teachers encountered in their own courses. Over time, SoTL practice reoriented to more collaborative inquiries and to partnerships with students. SoTL also began to be woven into the fabric of disciplines and institutions, including new journals and professional rewards and promotion criteria. Looking across that history, a multinational group of authors in 2016 concluded that "SoTL's richness is not in the model originally devised by Boyer, but in what it has become" (Fanghanel, Pritchard, Potter, Wisker, Locke, Healey, McConnell, Masika, McGowan, Parker, Clayton, Graham, Higgs, Coppola, Chalmers, Chick, Ciccone, and Bracegirdle 2016, 15).

In the decade since then, both in the field's evolution and in its responses to local and global changes over these years, SoTL has continued to "become." From today forward, you will be part of that becoming. As you close this book, we invite you to ask yourself where SoTL might guide you, and where you might guide SoTL.

Questions for You

We invite you to explore these questions in individual reflection or collegial conversation:
- What scholarly (or other) communities have you been part of that have contributed meaningfully to your work or life? What are the characteristics of those communities that you can seek out and cultivate in SoTL communities?
- Who do you—or who do you want to—have "significant conversations" with about teaching, learning, and inquiry? How can you expand and deepen those conversations? How can you invite others into those communities?
- In what ways do you want your career to develop in the future? What role(s) might SoTL play in that process?

Supplemental Materials

Video: This reflective module on exploring "your collegial context" provides research-informed guidance on having "significant conversations" and developing "significant networks" and "microcultures" to support your teaching and SoTL, featuring Katarina Mårtensson and Torgny Roxå from Lund University.

References

Abbot, Sophia. 2024. "SoTL Citizen: A Memoir of Home and Exile in the Scholarship of Teaching and Learning." In *Becoming a SoTL Scholar*, edited by Janice Miller-Young and Nancy L. Chick, 36–51. Elon Center for Engaged Learning.

Aby, Athulya. 2022. "Decolonisation of Architectural History Education in India." *Scholarship of Teaching and Learning in the South* 6 (3): 6–25. https://doi.org/10.36615/sotls.v6i3.268.

Adams, Maurianne, Lee Anne Bell, Diane J. Goodman, Davey Shlasko, Rachel R. Briggs, and Romina Pacheco. 2022. *Teaching for Diversity and Social Justice*. 4th ed. Routledge.

Aragón, Oriana R., Sarah L. Eddy, and Mark J. Graham. 2018. "Faculty Beliefs about Intelligence Are Related to the Adoption of Active-Learning Practices." *CBE—Life Sciences Education* 17 (3). https://doi.org/10.1187/cbe.17-05-0084.

Archer-Kuhn, Beth, Yeonjung Lee, Savannah Finnessey, and Jacky Liu. 2020. "Inquiry-Based Learning As a Facilitator to Student Engagement in Undergraduate and Graduate Social Work Programs." *Teaching & Learning Inquiry* 8 (1): 187–207. https://doi.org/10.20343/teachlearninqu.8.1.13.

Artze-Vega, Isis, Flower Darby, Bryan Dewsbury, and Mays Imad. 2023. *The Norton Guide to Equity-Minded Teaching*. W. W. Norton.

Baskerville, Delia and Helen Goldblatt. 2009. "Learning to Be a Critical Friend: From Professional Indifference through Challenge to Unguarded Conversations." *Cambridge Journal of Education* 39 (2): 205–221. https://doi.org/10.1080/03057640902902260.

Bass, Randy. 1999. "The Scholarship of Teaching: What's the Problem?" *inventio 1* (1): 1–10.

Bass, Randall. 2020. "What's the Problem Now?" *To Improve the Academy* 39 (1): 3–30. http://dx.doi.org/10.3998/tia.17063888.0039.102.

Bass, Randy and Bret Eynon. 2009. "Capturing the Visible Evidence of Invisible Learning." In *The Difference that Inquiry Makes: A Collaborative Case Study of Technology and Learning, from the Visible Knowledge Project*, edited by Randy Bass and Bret Eynon, 4–29.

Bass, Randy, and Sherry Lee Linkon. 2008. "On the Evidence of Theory: Close Reading as a Disciplinary Model for Writing about Teaching and Learning." *Arts and Humanities in Higher Education* 7 (3): 245–261. https://doi.org/10.1177/1474022208094410.

Becher, Tony and Paul R. Trowler. 2001. *Academic Tribes and Territories*. The Society for Research into Higher Education and Open University Press.

Behari-Leak, Kasturi. 2020. "Toward a Borderless, Decolonized, Socially Just, and Inclusive Scholarship of Teaching and Learning." *Teaching & Learning Inquiry* 8 (1): 4–23. https://doi.org/10.20343/teachlearninqu.8.1.2.

Behari-Leak, Kasturi. 2022. "Going Public With SoTL as Social Activism." In *Going Public Reconsidered: Engaging with the World Beyond Academe through the Scholarship of Teaching and Learning,* edited by Nancy L. Chick and Jennifer C. Friberg, 33–46. Stylus.

Berenson, Carol. 2018. "Identifying a Tradition of Inquiry: Articulating Research Assumptions." In *SoTL in Action: Illuminating Critical Moments of Practice,* edited by Nancy L. Chick, 42–52. Routledge.

Bessette, Lee Skallerup. 2022. "The Scholarship of Teaching and Learning and Traditional Media." In *Going Public Reconsidered: Engaging with the World Beyond Academe through the Scholarship of Teaching and Learning,* edited by Nancy L. Chick and Jennifer C. Friberg, 118–128. Stylus.

Bester, Johannes, and Erica Pretorius. 2022. "Linking Reflective and Authentic Learning: Encouraging Deeper Learning Experiences in a First-Year Civil Engineering Module at a University in South Africa." *Scholarship of Teaching and Learning in the South* 6 (3): 108–122.

Biggs, John. 2009. *Teaching for Quality Learning at University.* Society for Research into Higher Education and Open University Press.

Biggs, John and Catherine Tang. 2011. *Teaching for Quality Learning at University.* 4th ed. Society for Research into Higher Education and Open University Press.

Blaich, Charles, Kathleen Wise, and I. N. Crawfordsville. 2011. "The Wabash National Study: The Impact of Teaching Practices and Institutional Conditions on Student Growth." Paper presented at the annual meeting of the American Educational Research Association, New Orleans, LA.

Bloch-Schulman, Stephen. 2016. "A Critique of Methods in the Scholarship of Teaching and Learning in Philosophy." *Teaching & Learning Inquiry* 4 (1): 80–94. https://doi.org/10.20343/teachlearninqu.4.1.10.

Bloch-Schulman, Stephen, and Sherry Lee Linkon. 2016. "Scholarship of Teaching and Learning in the Arts and Humanities: Moving the Conversation Forward (Special Section Editors' Introduction)." *Teaching & Learning Inquiry* 4 (1): 52–54. https://doi.org/10.20343/teachlearninqu.4.1.7.

Bloch-Schulman, Stephen, Susan Wharton Conkling, Sherry Lee Linkon, Karen Manarin, and Kathleen Perkins. 2016. "Asking Bigger Questions: An Invitation to Further Conversation." *Teaching & Learning Inquiry* 4 (1): 108-14. https://doi.org/10.20343/teachlearninqu.4.1.12.

Booth, Shirley, and Lorenzo C. Woollacott. 2018."On the Constitution of SoTL: Its Domains and Contexts." *Higher Education* 75, 537–551. https://doi.org/10.1007/s10734-017-0156-7.

Bovill, Catherine. 2020. *Co-creating Learning and Teaching: Towards Relational Pedagogy in Higher Education.* Routledge. Critical Practice in Higher Education.

Boyd, Diane E. 2024. "Embracing Liminality," In *Threshold Concepts in the Moment*, edited by Jason P. Davies, Elia Gironacci, Susannah McGowan, Abel Nyamapfene, Julie Rattray, Anne M. Tierney, and Andrea S. Webb, 171–185. Brill. https://doi.org/10.1163/9789004680661.

Boyer, Ernest L. 1987. *College: The Undergraduate Experience in America.* Harper and Row.

Boyer, Ernest L. 1990. *Scholarship Reconsidered: The Priorities of the Professoriate.* Carnegie Foundation for the Advancement of Teaching.

Brod, Garvin. 2021. "Toward an Understanding of When Prior Knowledge Helps or Hinders Learning." *npj Science of Learning* 6 (24): 1–3. https://doi.org/10.1038/s41539-021-00103-w.

Brookfield, Stephen D. 2017. *Becoming a Critically Reflective Teacher*. 2nd ed. Wiley.

Brownell, Sara E., and Kimberly D. Tanner. 2012. "Barriers to Faculty Pedagogical Change: Lack of Training, Time, Incentives, and Tensions with Professional Identity?" *CBE–Life Sciences Education* 11, 339–346. https://doi.org/10.1187/cbe.12-09-0163.

Bunnell, Sarah L., Nancy L. Chick, Melanie J. Hamilton, Anna Santucci Leoni, and Cherie Woolmer. 2024. "Generations of SoTL Scholars: Transferable Lessons and New Possibilities." *Transformative Dialogues* 17 (1). https://doi.org/10.26209/td2024vol17iss11801.

Bunnell, Sarah L., Peter Felten, and Kelly E. Matthews. 2022. "Toward Trust in SoTL: The Role of Relational Ethics." In *Ethics and the Scholarship of Teaching and Learning*, 129–146. Springer International Publishing.

Bunnell, Sarah L., and Susannah McGowan. 2024. "The Ceremony of SoTL Welcome: The International Society for the Scholarship of Teaching and Learning as a Case Study." *Transformative Dialogues* 17 (1). https://doi.org/10.26209/td2024vol17iss11799.

Burke, Kenneth. 1941. *The Philosophy of Literary Form*. University of California Press.

Burkhard, Tanja. 2022. "Facing Post-Truth Conspiracies in the Classroom: A Black Feminist Autoethnography of Teaching for Liberation After the Summer of Racial Reckoning." *Departures in Qualitative Research* 11 (3): 24–39. https://doi.org/10.1525/dcqr.2022.11.3.24.

Burman, Mary E., and Audrey Kleinsasser. 2004. "Ethical Guidelines for Use of Student Work: Moving from Teaching's Invisibility toInquiry's Visibility in SoTL." *Journal of General Education* 53 (1): 59–79.

Calder, Lendol. 2006. "Uncoverage: Toward a Signature Pedagogy for the History Survey." *Journal of American History* 92 (4): 1358–1370. https://doi.org/10.2307/4485896.

Calder, Lendol, and Robert Williams. 2021. "Must Students Write History Essays?" *The Journal of American History* 107 (4): 926–941. https://doi.org/10.1093/jahist/jaaa464.

Cappello, Alicia, and Janice Miller-Young. 2020. "Who Are We Citing and How? A SoTL Citation Analysis." *Teaching & Learning Inquiry* 8 (2): 3–16. https://doi.org/10.20343/teachlearninqu.8.2.2.

Center for Engaged Learning. 2013. "Best Practices for Integrating Student Voices in SoTL." Video, 10:38. Elon University. https://www.centerforengagedlearning.org/aiovg_videos/best-practices-for-integrating-student-voices-in-sotl/.

Center for Engaged Learning. 2013. "Examples of SoTL Projects." Video, 5:00. Elon University and International Society for the Scholarship of Teaching and Learning. https://www.centerforengagedlearning.org/aiovg_videos/examples-of-sotl-projects.

Center for Engaged Learning. 2013. "Key Characteristics of SoTL." Video. Elon University and International Society for the Scholarship of Teaching and Learning. https://www.centerforengagedlearning.org/aiovg_videos/key-characteristics-of-the-scholarship-of-teaching-and-learning.

Center for Engaged Learning. 2013. "Pat Hutchings on the 'Taxonomy of Questions from the Intro to Opening Lines.'" Video, 3:48. Elon University. https://www.

centerforengagedlearning.org/studying-engaged-learning/asking-inquiry-questions.

Center for Engaged Learning. 2013. "Strategies for Going Public with SoTL." Video, 7:31. Elon University and International Society for the Scholarship of Teaching and Learning. https://www.centerforengagedlearning.org/aiovg_videos/strategies-for-going-public-with-sotl.

Center for Engaged Learning. 2014. "Janice Miller-Young on the Experience of Searching for SoTL Literature." Video, 6:24. Elon University. https://www.centerforengagedlearning.org/aiovg_videos/janice-miller-young-on-the-experience-of-searching-for-sotl-literature.

Center for Engaged Learning. 2014. "Olivia Choplin on the Experience of Searching for SoTL Literature." Video, 8:14. Elon University. https://www.centerforengagedlearning.org/aiovg_videos/olivia-choplin-on-the-experience-of-searching-for-sotl-literature.

Center for Engaged Learning. 2023. "Margy MacMillan on the SoTL Information Landscape." Video. Elon University. https://www.centerforengagedlearning.org/aiovg_videos/margy-macmillan-on-the-sotl-information-landscape.

Chaka, Chaka, Thembeka Shange, Sibusiso Ndlangamandla, and Dumisile Mkhize. 2022. "Situating Some Aspects of the Scholarship of Teaching and Learning (SoTL) in South African Higher Education Within Southern Theories." *Journal of Contemporary Issues in Education* 17 (2): 6–24. https://doi.org/10.20355/jcie29494.

Chan, Yuen Fook, Gurnam Kaur Sidhu, Narasuman Suthagar, Lai Fong Lee, and Bee Wah Yap. 2016. "Relationship of Inquiry-based Instruction on Active Learning in Higher

Education." *Pertanika Journal of Social Science & Humanities* 24, 55–72.

Chick, Nancy L., La Vonne Cornell-Swanson, Katina Lazarides, and Renee Meyers. 2014. "Reconciling Apples & Oranges: A Constructivist SoTL Writing Program." *International Journal for the Scholarship of Teaching and Learning* 8 (2): 1–42. https://doi.org/10.20429/ijsotl.2014.080213.

Chick, Nancy L. 2013. "Difference, Power, and Privilege in the Scholarship of Teaching and Learning: The Value of Humanities SoTL." In *SoTL In and Across the Disciplines*, edited by Kathleen McKinney, 15–33. Indiana University Press.

Chick, Nancy L. 2017. "Does Reading SoTL Matter?: On Difficult Questions of Impact." *InSight: A Journal of Scholarly Teaching* 12: 9–13. https://doi.org/10.46504/12201700ch.

Chick, Nancy, Sarah Bunnell, Peter Felten, Bettie Higgs, Aaron Long, Karen Manarin, Beth Marquis, Katarina Mårtensson, Kelly Matthews, Jessie L. Moore, and Lauren Scharff. 2017. "ISSOTL Conference Pedagogy." *ISSOTL*. https://issotl.com/issotl-conference-pedagogy.

Chick, Nancy L. 2018. "An Origin Story." *National Teaching and Learning Forum* 27 (6): 7–8.

Chick, Nancy. 2019a. "Strategies for Ethical SoTL Practice." In *The National Teaching & Learning Forum* 28 (96): 7–10. https://doi.org/10.1002/ntlf.30216.

Chick, Nancy. 2019b. "How to Start Doing SoTL." *National Teaching and Learning Forum* 28 (2): 10–11. https://doi.org/10.1002/ntlf.30189.

Chick, Nancy. 2023. "Demystifying SoTL, Part II." *ChickChat*, May 6. https://nancychick.wordpress.com/2023/05/06/demystifying-sotl-part-ii/.

Chick, Nancy L., Sophia Abbot, Lucy Mercer-Mapstone, Christopher P. Ostrowdun, and Krista Grensavitch. 2021. "Naming Is Power: Citation Practices in SoTL." *Teaching & Learning Inquiry* 9 (2). https://doi.org/10.20343/teachlearninqu.9.2.2.

Chick, Nancy L., Laura Cruz, Jennifer C. Friberg, and Hillary H. Steiner. 2023. "Making Space for Failure in the Scholarship of Teaching and Learning: A Blueprint." *Teaching & Learning Inquiry* 11. https://doi.org/10.20343/teachlearninqu.11.36.

Chick, Nancy. 2024. "Engaging in Nuance: Authentic SoTL Engagement for Scholars in the Humanities." In *Becoming a SoTL Scholar*, edited by Janice Miller-Young and Nancy L. Chick, 126–156. Center for Engaged Learning.

Chick, Nancy L., Holly Hassel, and Aeron Haynie. 2009. "'Pressing an Ear Against the Hive': Reading Literature for Complexity." *Pedagogy* 9 (3): 399–422. https://doi.org/10.1215/15314200-2009-003.

Chick, Nancy L., and Jennifer C. Friberg. 2022. *Going Public Reconsidered: Engaging with the World Beyond Academe through the Scholarship of Teaching and Learning*. Stylus.

Chick, Nancy L. 2024. "'Dear Author': A Transparent SoTL Peer Review." *Transformative Dialogues* 17 (1): 91–99. https://doi.org/10.26209/td2024vol17iss11800.

Chick, Nancy L. 2025. "SoTL Posters." In *An Applied Introduction to the Scholarship of Teaching and Learning*, edited by Shannon M. Sipes, Nancy L. Chick, and Laura Cruz. Indiana University Press.

Chng, Huang Hoon, and Peter Looker. 2013. "On the Margins of SoTL Discourse: An Asian Perspective." *Teaching & Learning Inquiry* 1 (1): 131–145. https://doi.org/10.20343/teachlearninqu.1.1.131.

Chng, Huang Hoon, Katarina Mårtensson, and Brenda Leibowitz. 2020. "Leading Change from Different Shores: The Challenges of Contextualizing the Scholarship of Teaching and Learning". *Teaching & Learning Inquiry* 8 (1): 24–41. https://doi.org/10.20343/teachlearninqu.8.1.3.

Ciccone, Anthony. 2018. "Learning Matters: Asking Meaningful Questions." In *SoTL in Action: Illuminating Critical Moments of Practice,* edited by Nancy L. Chick, 15–22. Stylus.

Cook-Sather, Alison, and Morgan Cook-Sather. 2023. "From Reporting to Removing Barriers: Toward Transforming Accommodation Culture into Equity Culture." *Education Sciences* 13 (6): 611. https://doi.org/10.3390/educsci13060611.

Cook-Sather, Alison, Sophia Abbot, and Peter Felten. 2019. "Legitimating Reflective Writing in SoTL: 'Dysfunctional Illusions of Rigor' Revisited". *Teaching & Learning Inquiry* 7 (2):14–27. https://doi.org/10.20343/teachlearninqu.7.2.2.

Cooper, Katelyn M., and Sara E. Brownell. 2016. "Coming Out in Class: Challenges and Benefits of Active Learning in a Biology Classroom for LGBTQIA Students." *CBE—Life Sciences Education* 15 (3): 1–19. https://doi.org/10.1187/cbe.16-01-0074.

Cappello, Alicia, and Janice Miller-Young. 2020. "Who Are We Citing and How? A SoTL Citation Analysis". *Teaching & Learning Inquiry* 8 (2): 3–16. https://doi.org/10.20343/teachlearninqu.8.2.2.

Corrigan, Paul T. 2019. "Threshold Concepts in Literary Studies." *Teaching & Learning Inquiry* 7 (1): 3–17. https://doi.org/10.20343/teachlearninqu.7.1.2.

Corwin, Lisa A., Michael E. Ramsey, Eric A. Vance, Elizabeth Woolner, Stevie Maiden, Nina Gustafson, and Joseph A. Harsh. 2022. "Students' Emotions, Perceived Coping, and

Outcomes in Response to Research-Based Challenges and Failures in Two Sequential CUREs." *CBE—Life Sciences Education* 21 (2). https://doi.org/10.1187/cbe.21-05-0131.

Cousin, Glynis. 2009. *Researching Learning in Higher Education: An Introduction to Contemporary Methods and Approaches*. Routledge.

Cox, Rebecca D. 2011. *The College Fear Factor: How Students and Professors Misunderstand One Another*. Harvard University Press.

Cruz, Laura, and Eileen Grodziak. 2021. "SoTL Under Stress: Rethinking Teaching and Learning Scholarship During a Global Pandemic." *Teaching & Learning Inquiry* 9 (1): 3–12. https://doi.org/10.20343/teachlearninqu.9.1.2.

Divan, Aysha, Lynn O. Ludwig, Kelly E. Matthews, Phillip M. Motley, and Ana M. Tomljenovic-Berube. 2017. "Survey of Research Approaches Utilised in the Scholarship of Teaching and Learning Publications." *Teaching & Learning Inquiry* 5 (2): 16–29. https://doi.org/10.20343/teachlearninqu.5.2.3.

Drummond, Tom, and Kayln Shea Owens. 2010. "Capturing Students' Learning." In *Engaging Student Voices in the Study of Teaching and Learning*, edited by Carmen Werder and Megan M. Otis, 162–184. Stylus.

Eady, Michelle J. 2024. "Cultivating International Collaborations Towards Sustained SoTL Engagement." In *Becoming a SoTL Scholar*, edited by Janice Miller-Young and Nancy L. Chick, 256–265. Center for Engaged Learning.

Fallon, Dianne. 2006. "'Lucky to Live in Maine': Examining Student Responses to Diversity Issues." *Teaching English in the Two-Year College* 33 (4): 410–420.

Fanghanel, Joëlle. 2013. "Going Public With Pedagogical Inquiries: SoTL As a Methodology for Faculty Professional

Development." *Teaching & Learning Inquiry* 1 (1): 59–70. https://doi.org/10.20343/teachlearninqu.1.1.59.

Fanghanel, Joëlle, Jane Pritchard, Jacqueline Potter, Gina Wisker, William Locke, Mick Healey, Catherine McConnell, Rachel Masika, Susannah McGowan, Pam Parker, Sue Clayton, Hilaire Graham, Bettie Higgs, Brian P. Coppola, Denise Chalmers, Nancy Chick, Anthony Ciccone, and Luke Bracegirdle. 2016. *Defining and Supporting the Scholarship of Teaching and Learning (SoTL): A Sector-wide Study.* Higher Education Academy. https://www.advance-he.ac.uk/knowledge-hub/defining-and-supporting-scholarship-teaching-and-learning-sotl-sector-wide-study.

Fedoruk, Lisa M., ed. *Ethics and the Scholarship of Teaching and Learning.* Vol. 2. Springer Nature.

Felten, Peter. 2005. "'Photos–The Almost Most Objective Evidence There Is': Reading Words and Images of the 1960s." *Reader* 52: 38–53.

Felten, Peter. 2013. "Principles of Good Practice in SoTL." *Teaching & Learning Inquiry* 1 (1): 121–25. https://doi.org/10.20343/teachlearninqu.1.1.121.

Felten, Peter, and Johan Geertsema. 2023. "Recovering the Heart of SoTL: Inquiring into Teaching and Learning 'As If the World Mattered.'" *Innovative Higher Education* 48 (6): 1095–1112. https://doi.org/10.1007/s10755-023-09675-4.

Felten, Peter, and Leo M. Lambert. 2020. *Relationship-Rich Education. How Human Connections Drive Success in College.* John Hopkins University Press.

Fielding, Michael and others. 1999. "Radical Collegiality: Affirming Teaching as an Inclusive Professional Practice." *Australian Educational Researcher* 26 (2): 1–65. https://search.informit.org/doi/10.3316/ielapa.200006486.

Fisher, Matthew A. 2024. "Guiding Practices for STEM Faculty Interested in SoTL." In *Becoming a SoTL Scholar*, edited by Janice Miller-Young and Nancy L. Chick, 104–125. Center for Engaged Learning.

Fjelkner Pihl, Annika. 2022. *Building Study-Related Relationships: How Student Relationships and Readiness Affect Academic Outcome in Higher Education.* PhD diss., Lund University, Faculty of Engineering, Centre for Engineering Education. https://researchportal.hkr.se/ws/portalfiles/portal/51591994/Annika_Fjelkner_Pihl_HELA.pdf.

Flaherty, Colleen. 2020. "Burning Out." *Inside Higher Education,* September 13, 2020. https://www.insidehighered.com/news/2020/09/14/faculty-members-struggle-burnout.

Freeman, Scott, Sarah L. Eddy, Miles McDonough, Michelle K. Smith, Nnadozie Okoroafor, Hannah Jordt, and Mary Pat Wenderoth. 2014. "Active Learning Increases Student Performance in Science, Engineering, and Mathematics." *Proceedings of the National Academy of Sciences* 111 (23): 8410–8415.

Friberg, Jennifer. 2016. "The Students-As-Partners in SoTL Movement: Wonderments from ISSoTL." *The SoTL Advocate* (blog). October 31, 2016. https://illinoisstateuniversitysotl.wordpress.com/2016/10/31/the-students-as-partners-in-sotl-movement-wonderments-from-issotl/.

Friberg, Jennifer C., Lauren Scharff, John Draeger, and Aaron S. Richmond. 2022. "Making Scholarship of Teaching and Learning Public Using Weblogs." In *Going Public Reconsidered: Engaging with the World Beyond Academe through the Scholarship of Teaching and Learning,* edited by Nancy L. Chick and Jennifer C. Friberg, 104–117. Stylus.

Gale, Richard. 2009. "Asking Questions that Matter… Asking Questions of Value." *International Journal for the Scholarship *of Teaching and Learning* 3 (2). https://doi.org/10.20429/ijsotl.2009.030203.

Gayle, Barbara M., Nancy Randall, Lin Langley, and Raymond Preiss. 2013. "Faculty Learning Processes: A Model for Moving from Scholarly Teaching to the Scholarship of Teaching and Learning." *Teaching & Learning Inquiry* 1 (1): 81–93. https://doi.org/10.20343/teachlearninqu.1.1.81.

Geertz, Clifford. 1973. *The Interpretation of Cultures*. Basic Books.

Gillespie, Bruce, Michelle Goodridge, and Shirley Hall. 2024. "Reaching Across the Disciplines to Build a Grassroots SoTL Community." In *Becoming a SoTL Scholar*, edited by Janice Miller-Young and Nancy L. Chick, 187–201. Center for Engaged Learning.

Glassick, Charles E., Mary Taylor Huber, and Gene I. Maeroff. 1997. *Scholarship Assessed: Evaluation of the Professoriate*. Jossey-Bass.

Godbold, Nattalia, Dawne Irving-Bell, Jill McSweeney-Flaherty, Patrice Torcivia, Lauren Schlesselman, and Heather Smith. 2021. "The Courage to SoTL." *Teaching & Learning Inquiry* 9 (1): 380–94. https://doi.org/10.20343/teachlearninqu.9.1.25.

Graff, Gerald, and Cathy Birkenstein. 2021. *They Say / I Say: The Moves that Matter in Academic Writing*. W. W. Norton & Company.

Green, Corinne A. 2024. "The Braided Threads of Learning, Changing, and Becoming: Reflections on My SoTL Adventures (So Far)." In *Becoming a SoTL Scholar*, edited by Janice Miller-Young and Nancy L. Chick, 52–66. Center for Engaged Learning.

Green, Corinne A., Michelle J. Eady, Marian McCarthy, Ashley B. Akenson, Briony Supple, Jacinta McKeon, and James G. R. Cronin. 2020. "Beyond the Conference: Singing Our

SSONG." *Teaching & Learning Inquiry* 8 (1): 42–60. https://doi.org/10.20343/teachlearninqu.8.1.4.

Haigh, Neil, and Andrew J. Withell. 2020. "The Place of Research Paradigms in SoTL Practice: An Inquiry." *Teaching & Learning Inquiry* 8 (2). http://dx.doi.org/10.20343/teachlearninqu.8.2.3.

Halpern, Faye. 2023. "The Morphology of the SoTL Article: New Possibilities for the Stories That SoTL Scholars Tell About Teaching and Learning." *Teaching & Learning Inquiry* 11: 1–23. https://doi.org/10.20343/teachlearninqu.11.8.

Hamilton, Melanie, and Brett McCollum. 2024. "Moving From 'Good' to 'Great' SoTL: The Importance of Describing Your Research Epistemological and Ontological Traditions in Your SoTL Scholarship." *Teaching & Learning Inquiry* 12, 1–15. https://doi.org/10.20343/teachlearninqu.12.31.

Handal, Gunnar. 1999. "Consultation Using Critical Friends." *New Directions for Teaching & Learning* 79: 59–70. https://doi.org/10.1002/tl.7907.

Harlap, Yael, and Hanne Riese. 2022. "'We Don't Throw Stones, We Throw Flowers': Race Discourse and Race Evasiveness in the Norwegian University Classroom." *Ethnic and Racial Studies* 45 (7): 1218–1238. https://doi.org/10.1080/01419870.2021.1904146.

Hassel, Holly, and Joanne Giordano. 2009. "Transfer Institutions, Transfer of Knowledge: The Development of Rhetorical Adaptability and Underprepared Writers." *Teaching English in the Two-Year College* 37 (1): 24–40. https://doi.org/10.58680/tetyc20097731.

Healey, Mick, Kelly E. Matthews, and Alison Cook-Sather. 2020. *Writing about Learning and Teaching in Higher Education*

Creating and Contributing to Scholarly Conversations across a Range of Genres. Center for Engaged Learning.

Healey, Mick, and Ruth Healey. 2023. "Reviewing the Literature on Scholarship of Teaching and Learning (SoTL): An Academic Literacies Perspective: Part 2." *Teaching & Learning Inquiry* 11. https://doi.org/10.20343/teachlearninqu.11.5.

Healey, Ruth L., Tina Bass, Jay Caulfield, Adam Hoffman, Michelle K. McGinn, Janice Miller-Young, and Martin Haigh. 2013. "Being Ethically Minded: Practising the Scholarship of Teaching and Learning in an Ethical Manner." *Teaching & Learning Inquiry* 1 (2): 23–32. https://doi.org/10.2979/teachlearninqu.1.2.23.

Hersch, Gil. "Educational Equipoise and the Educational Misconception: Lessons from Bioethics." *Teaching & Learning Inquiry* 6 (2): 3–15. https://doi.org/10.20343/teachlearninqu.6.2.2.

Hewson, Kelly and Lee Easton. 2022. "Packing Up the Big Tent: Que(e)rying and Decolonizing SoTL." *Imagining SoTL* 2 (1). https://doi.org/10.29173/isotl602.

Hill, Jennifer, Kathy Berlin, Julia Choate, Lisa Cravens-Brown, Lisa McKendrick-Calder, and Susan Smith. 2021. "Exploring the Emotional Responses of Undergraduate Students to Assessment Feedback: Implications for Instructors." *Teaching & Learning Inquiry* 9 (1): 294–316. https://doi.org/10.20343/teachlearninqu.9.1.20.

Holec, Victoria, and Richelle Marynowski. 2020. "Does It Matter Where You Teach? Insights from a Quasi-Experimental Study of Student Engagement in an Active Learning Classroom." *Teaching & Learning Inquiry* 8 (2). http://dx.doi.org/10.20343/teachlearninqu.8.2.10.

Hovland, Ingie. 2021. "The Importance of Making-While-Reading for Undergraduate Readers: An Example of Inductive

SoTL." *Teaching & Learning Inquiry* 9 (1): 27–44. https://doi.org/10.20343/teachlearninqu.9.1.4.

Huber, Mary Taylor, and Pat Hutchings. 2005. *The Advancement of Learning: Building the Teaching Commons*. Jossey-Bass.

Huber, Mary Taylor, and Sherwyn P. Morreale, eds. 2002. *Disciplinary Styles in the Scholarship of Teaching and Learning: Exploring Common Ground*. American Association for Higher Education and Carnegie Foundation for the Advancement of Teaching.

Huijser, Henk, Janel Seeley, and James Cronin. 2023. "International Collaborative Writing Groups and Public SoTL." *ISSOTL* (blog), January 11, 2023.

Hutchings, Pat. 2000. *Opening Lines: Approaches to the Scholarship of Teaching and Learning*. Carnegie Foundation for the Advancement of Teaching.

Jardine, Hannah Elizabeth, Gavin Frome, and Elizabeth Campbell Griffith. 2023. "Partnering with Students to Redesign an Introductory Chemistry Laboratory Course: An Exploration of the Process and Implications." *International Journal for Students as Partners* 7 (1): 161–171. https://doi.org/10.15173/ijsap.v7i1.5260.

Johansson, Ingela. 2012. Ökad kontakttid med ämnet – exempel från språkutbildning. *högre utbildning* 2 (2): 123–128. https://hogreutbildning.se/index.php/hu/article/view/838.

Kandiko, Camille, David Hay, and Saranne Weller. 2013. "Concept Mapping in the Humanities to Facilitate Reflection: Externalizing the Relationship between Public and Personal Learning." *Arts and Humanities in Higher Education* 12 (1): 70–87. https://doi.org/10.1177/1474022211399381.

Kapur, Manu. 2016. "Examining Productive Failure, Productive Success, Unproductive Failure, and Unproductive Success in

Learning." *Educational Psychologist* 51 (2): 289–299. https://doi.org/10.1080/00461520.2016.1155457.

Keogh, Bryn, Lorelli Nowell, Eleftheria Laios, Lisa McKendrick-Calder, Whitney Lucas Molitor, and Kerry Wilbur. 2024. "Using Infographics to Go Public With SoTL." *Teaching & Learning Inquiry* 12. https://doi.org/10.20343/teachlearninqu.12.10.

Kreber, Carolin. 2013. "The Transformative Potential of the Scholarship of Teaching." *Teaching & Learning Inquiry* 1 (1): 5–18. https://doi.org/10.20343/teachlearninqu.1.1.5.

Kreber, Carolin. 2013a. "Empowering the Scholarship of Teaching: An Arendtian and Critical Perspective." *Studies in Higher Education* 38 (6): 857–869.

Kreber, Carolin. 2002. "Teaching Excellence, Teaching Expertise, and the Scholarship of Teaching." *Innovation Higher Education* 27 (1): 5–23. https://doi.org/10.1023/A:1020464222360.

Kuh, George D. 2003. "What We're Learning About Student Engagement From NSSE: Benchmarks for Effective Educational Practices." *Change: The Magazine of Higher Learning* 35 (2): 24–32. https://doi.org/10.1080/00091380309604090.

Kumar, Rita, and Brenda Refaei. 2021. *Equity and Inclusion in Higher Education: Strategies for Teaching*. University of Cincinnati Press.

Larsson, Maria, Katarina Mårtensson, Linda Price, and Torgny Roxå. 2020. "Constructive Friction? Charting the Relation Between Educational Research and the Scholarship of Teaching and Learning." *Teaching & Learning Inquiry* 8 (1): 61–75. https://doi.org/10.20343/teachlearninqu.8.1.5.

Lee, See Wong, Sookweon Min, and Geoffrey P. Mamerow. 2015. "Pygmalion in the Classroom and the Home: Expectation's Role in the Pipeline to STEMM."

Teachers College Record 117 (9): 1–40. https://doi.org/10.1177/016146811511700907.

Leibowitz, Brenda. 2010. "Towards SoTL as Critical Engagement: A Perspective from the 'South.'" *International Journal for the Scholarship of Teaching and Learning* 4 (2): 1–5. https://doi.org/10.20429/ijsotl.2010.040207.

Leiter, Michael P., Phyllis Harvie, and Cindy Frizzell. 1998. "The Correspondence of Patient Satisfaction and Nurse Burnout." *Social Science & Medicine* 47 (10): 1611–1617. https://doi.org/10.1016/S0277-9536(98)00207-X.

Leiter, Michael P., and Christina Maslach. 2009. "Nurse Turnover: The Mediating Role of Burnout." *Journal of Nursing Management* 17 (3): 331–339. https://doi.org/10.1111/j.1365-2834.2009.01004.x.

Li, Jin. 2009. "Learning to Self-Perfect: Chinese Beliefs about Learning." In *Revisiting the Chinese Learner: Changing Contexts, Changing Education*, edited by Carol K. K. Chan and Nirmala Rao, 35–70. Springer.

Lindberg-Sand, Åsa, and Anders Sonesson. 2008. "Compulsory Higher Education Teacher Training in Sweden: Development of a National Standards Framework Based on the Scholarship of Teaching and Learning." *Tertiary Education and Management* 14 (2): 123–139. https://doi.org/10.1080/13583880802053051.

Linkon, Sherry. 2000. "Students' Perspectives on Interdisciplinary Learning." In *Opening Lines: Approaches to the Scholarship of Teaching and Learning*, edited by Pat Hutchings, 63–71. Carnegie Foundation for the Advancement of Teaching.

Linkon, Sherry. 2011. *Literary Learning: Teaching the English Major*. Indiana University Press.

Loukopoulou, Katarina. 2022. "Third Space Reloaded: Reflections from the Academic Development Front." *Third Space Perspectives – Exploring Integrated Practice* (blog), September 29, 2022. https://www.thirdspaceperspectives.com/blog/thirdspacerebooted.

Lovett, Marsha C., Michael W. Bridges, Michele DiPietro, Susan A. Ambrose, and Marie K. Norman. 2023. *How Learning Works: 8 Research-Based Principles for Smart Teaching*. Jossey-Bass/Wiley.

Macfarlane, Bruce. 2004. *Teaching with Integrity: The Ethics of Higher Education Practice*. Routledge.

MacMillan, Margy. 2016. "Decode Yourself: Mine Your Research History to Help Plan Your Future SoTL Research." Paper presented at the Symposium on the Scholarship of Teaching and Learning, Banff, Alberta, Canada, November 10.

MacMillan, Margy. 2018. "Literature Review: Exploring New Territory." In *SoTL in Action: Illuminating Critical Moments of Practice*, edited by Nancy L. Chick, 23–41. Stylus.

Manarin, Karen. 2016. "Interpreting Undergraduate Research Posters in the Literature Classroom." *Teaching & Learning Inquiry* 4 (1): 55–69. https://doi.org/10.20343/teachlearninqu.4.1.8.

Manarin, Karen. 2017. "Reading the Stories of Teaching and Learning—ISSOTL 2016 Opening Keynote." *Teaching & Learning Inquiry* 5 (1): 164–71. https://doi.org/10.20343/teachlearninqu.5.1.13.

Manarin, Karen. 2018. "Close Reading: Paying Attention to Student Artifacts." In *SoTL in Action: Illuminating Critical Moments of Practice*, edited by Nancy L. Chick, 100–108. Stylus.

Manarin, Karen, Christine Adams, Richard Fendler, Heidi Marsh, Ethan Pohl, Suzanne Porath, and Alison Thomas. 2021. "Examining the Focus of SoTL Literature—Teaching and Learning?" *Teaching & Learning Inquiry* 9 (1): 349–364.

Mårtensson, Katarina, and Torgny Roxå. 2016. "Peer Engagement for Teaching and Learning: Competence, Autonomy and Social Solidarity in Academic Microcultures." *Uniped* 39 (2): 131–143. https://doi.org/10.18261/issn.1893-8981-2016-02-04.

Mårtensson, Katarina, Torgny Roxå, and Thomas Olsson. 2011. "Developing a Quality Culture through the Scholarship of Teaching and Learning." *Higher Education Research and Development* 30 (1): 51–62. https://doi.org/10.1080/07294360.2011.536972.

Martin, Ryan C. 2018. "Respect, Justice, and Doing Good." In *SoTL in Action: Illuminating Critical Moments of Practice*, edited by Nancy L. Chick, 100–108. Stylus.

Mashiyi, Nomakhaya Fidelia. 2018. "Integrating Inquiry-Based Learning into the Academic Literacy Course to Enhance Student Learning." *Scholarship of Teaching and Learning in the South* 2 (2): 37–52. https://doi.org/10.36615/sotls.v2i2.33.

Mason, Derritt. 2021. "I Suck at This Game: 'Let's Play' Videos, Think-Alouds, and the Pedagogy of Bad Feelings." *Teaching & Learning Inquiry* 9 (1): 200–217. https://doi.org/10.20343/teachlearninqu.9.1.14.

Matthews, Kelly E. 2019. "Rethinking the Problem of Faculty Resistance to Engaging with Students as Partners in Learning and Teaching in Higher Education." *International Journal for the Scholarship of Teaching and Learning* 13 (2): 1–5. https://doi.org/10.20429/ijsotl.2019.130202.

Maurer, Trent W. 2018. "Methods and Measures Matter: Meaningful Questionnaires." In *SoTL in Action: Illuminating Critical Moments of Practice*, edited by Nancy L. Chick, 71–81. Stylus.

Maurer, Trent W., Cherie Woolmer, Nichole L. Powell, Carol Sisson, Catherine Snelling, Odd Rune Stalheim, and Ian J. Turner. 2021. "Sharing SoTL Findings With Students: An Intentional Knowledge Mobilization Strategy." *Teaching & Learning Inquiry* 9 (1): 333–48. https://doi.org/10.20343/teachlearninqu.9.1.22.

McCollum, Brett M., Lisa Regier, Jaque Leong, Sarah Simpson, and Shayne Sterner. 2014. "The Effects of Using Touch-Screen Devices on Students' Molecular Visualization and Representational Competence Skills." *Journal of Chemical Education* 91 (11): 1810–1817. https://doi.org/10.1021/ed400674v.

McCarthy, Marian. 2024. "Building Transdisciplinary SoTL: Creating a Culture and Language of Listening and Learning for Understanding." *Transformative Dialogues* 17 (1): 100–118. https://doi.org/10.26209/td2024vol17iss11810.

McIntosh, Emily, and Diane Nutt. 2022. *The Impact of the Integrated Practitioner in Higher Education: Studies in Third Space Professionalism*. Routledge.

McSweeney, Jill and Schnurr, Matthew A. 2023. "Can SoTL Generate High Quality Research while Maintaining Its Commitment to Inclusivity?" *International Journal for the Scholarship of Teaching and Learning* 17 (1). https://doi.org/10.20429/ijsotl.2023.17104.

Mercer-Mapstone, Lucy, and Sophia Abbot. 2020. *The Power of Partnership: Students, Staff, and Faculty Revolutionizing Higher Education*. Center for Engaged Learning.

Miller-Young, Janice E., Catherine Anderson, Deborah Kiceniuk, Julie Mooney, Jessica Riddell, Alice Schmidt Hanbidge, Veronica Ward, Maureen A. Wideman, and Nancy Chick. 2017. "Leading Up in the Scholarship of Teaching and Learning." *The Canadian Journal for the Scholarship of Teaching and Learning* 8 (2): 1–14. https://doi.org/10.5206/cjsotl-rcacea.2017.2.4.

Miller-Young, Janice, and Michelle Yeo. 2015. "Conceptualizing and Communicating SoTL: A Framework for the Field." *Teaching & Learning Inquiry* 3 (2): 37–53. https://doi.org/10.20343/teachlearninqu.3.2.37.

Miller-Young, Janice E, and Nancy L. Chick, eds. 2024. *Becoming a SoTL Scholar*. Center for Engaged Learning.

Mills, David, and Mary Taylor Huber. 2005. "Anthropology and the Educational 'Trading Zone' Disciplinarity, Pedagogy and Professionalism." *Arts and Humanities in Higher Education* 4 (1): 9–32.

Moore, Jessie L. 2023. *Key Practices for Fostering Engaged Learning: A Guide for Faculty and Staff*. Routledge.

Moore, Jessie, Claire Hamshire, and Peter Felten. 2022. "Social Media and Public SoTL." In *Going Public Reconsidered: Engaging with the World Beyond Academe through the Scholarship of Teaching and Learning*, edited by Nancy L. Chick and Jennifer C. Friberg, 89–103. Stylus.

Mueller, Robin. 2018. "Ensuring Design Alignment in SoTL Inquiry: Merging Research Purpose and Methods." In *SoTL in Action: Illuminating Critical Moments of Practice,* edited by Nancy L. Chick, 53–61. Stylus.

National Academies of Sciences, Engineering, and Medicine. 2018. *How People Learn II: Learners, Contexts, and*

Cultures. The National Academies Press. https://doi.org/10.17226/24783.

National Academies of Sciences, Engineering, and Medicine. 2019. *Taking Action Against Clinician Burnout: A Systems Approach to Professional Well-Being.* The National Academies Press. https://doi.org/10.17226/25521.

NIH (National Institutes of Health). n.d. "Enhancing Reproducibility through Rigor and Transparency." *Policy & Compliance.* Accessed June 3, 2025. https://grants.nih.gov/policy-and-compliance/policy-topics/reproducibility.

Ndofirepi, Elizabeth Sipiwe, Raazia Moosa, Maureen J. Reed, and Mandivavarira Maodzwa-Taruvinga. 2023. "Perceived Life Balance, Cultural Experience, and Academic Outcomes: A Comparative Study of First-Generation Students in South Africa and Canada." *Scholarship of Teaching and Learning in the South* 7 (2): 21–45. https://journals.uj.ac.za/SOTL/index.php/sotls/article/view/284/152.

Nelson, Craig E. 1996. "Student Diversity Requires Different Approaches to College Teaching, Even in Math and Science." *American Behavioral Scientist* 40 (2): 165–175. https://doi.org/10.1177/0002764296040002007.

Nelson, Craig E. 2010. "Dysfunctional Illusions of Rigor: Lessons from the Scholarship of Teaching and Learning." *To Improve the Academy* 28 (1): 177–192. https://doi.org/10.1002/j.2334-4822.2010.tb00602.x.

Ng, Laura, and Mary A., Carney. 2017. "Scholarly Personal Narrative in the SoTL Tent." *Teaching & Learning Inquiry* 5 (1): 133–45. https://doi.org/10.20343/teachlearninqu.5.1.10.

O'Meara, KerryAnn, Aimee LaPointe Terosky, and Anna Neumann. 2008. *Faculty Careers and Work Lives: A Professional Growth Perspective.* Jossey-Bass.

Pace, David. 2004. "The Amateur in the Operating Room: History and the Scholarship of Teaching and Learning." *The American Historical Review* 109 (4): 1171–1192. https://doi.org/10.1086/530753.

Parker-Shandal, Crystena. 2023. "Participation in Higher Education Classroom Discussions: How Students' Identities Influence Perspective Taking and Engagement." *Teaching & Learning Inquiry* 11. https://doi.org/10.20343/teachlearninqu.11.19.

Parkman, Anna. 2016. "The Imposter Phenomenon in Higher Education: Incidence and Impact." *Journal of Higher Education Theory and Practice* 16 (1): 51–60.

Pfeifer, Mariel A., Julio J. Cordero, and Julie Dangremond Stanton. 2022. "What I Wish My Instructor Knew: How Active Learning Influences the Classroom Experiences and Self-Advocacy of STEM Majors with ADHD and Specific Learning Disabilities." *CBE—Life Sciences Education* 22 (1). https://doi.org/10.1187/cbe.21-12-0329.

Pleschová, Gabriela, Torgny Roxå, Kate Eileen Thomson, and Peter Felten. 2021. "Conversations That Make Meaningful Change in Teaching, Teachers, and Academic Development." *International Journal for Academic Development* 26 (3): 201–209. https://doi.org/10.1080/1360144X.2021.1958446.

Pleschová, Gabriela, Kathryn A. Sutherland, Peter Felten, Rachel Forsyth and Mary C. Wright. 2025. "Trust Building as Inherent to Academic Development Practice." *International Journal for Academic Development* 30 (1): 1–13. https://doi.org/10.1080/1360144X.2025.2454704.

Poole, Gary. 2018. "Using Intuition, Anecdote, and Observation: Rich Sources of SoTL Projects." In *SoTL in Action:*

Illuminating Critical Moments of Practice, edited by Nancy L. Chick, 21–28. Stylus.

Poole, Gary. 2013. "Square One: What Is Research?" In *The Scholarship of Teaching and Learning In and Across the Disciplines*, edited by Kathleen McKinney, 135–151. Indiana University Press.

Poole, Gary, and Nancy Chick. 2022. "Great Introspections: How and Why SoTL Looks Inward." *Teaching & Learning Inquiry* 10: 1–12. https://doi.org/10.20343/teachlearninqu.10.18.

Pope-Ruark, Rebecca. 2022. *Unraveling Faculty Burnout: Pathways to Reckoning and Renewal.* Johns Hopkins University Press.

Popovic, Celia, and David A. Green. 2012. *Understanding Undergraduates: Challenging Our Preconceptions of Student Success.* Routledge.

Potter, Michael K., and Brad Wuetherick. 2015. "Who Is Represented in the Teaching Commons?: SoTL Through the Lenses of the Arts and Humanities." *The Canadian Journal for the Scholarship of Teaching and Learning* 6 (2). https://doi.org/10.5206/cjsotl-rcacea.2015.2.2.

Razon, Selen, Jeannine Turner, Tristan E. Johnson, Guler Arsal, and Gershon Tenenbaum. 2012. "Effects of a Collaborative Annotation Method on Students' Learning and Learning-Related Motivation and Affect." *Computers in Human Behavior* 28 (2): 350–359. https://doi.org/10.1016/j.chb.2011.10.004.

Rosenthal, Robert, and Lenore Jacobson. 1968. "Pygmalion in the Classroom." *The Urban Review* 3, 16–20. https://doi.org/10.1007/BF02322211.

Roxå, Torgny and Katarina Mårtensson. 2009. "Significant Conversations and Significant Networks: Exploring the Backstage of the Teaching Arena." *Studies in Higher Education* 34 (5): 547–559. https://doi.org/10.1080/03075070802597200.

Roxå, Torgny, and Katarina Mårtensson. 2015. "Microcultures and Informal Learning: A Heuristic Guiding Analysis of Conditions for Informal Learning in Local Higher Education Workplaces." *International Journal for Academic Development* 20 (2): 193–205. https://doi.org/10.1080/1360144X.2015.1029929.

Roxå, Torgny, Thomas Olsson, and Katarina Mårtensson. 2008. "Appropriate Use of Theory in the Scholarship of Teaching and Learning as a Strategy for Institutional Development." *Arts and Humanities in Higher Education* 7 (3): 276–294. https://doi.org/10.1177/1474022208094412.

Salvatori, Mariolina. 2000. "Difficulty: The Great Educational Divide." In *Opening Lines: Approaches to the Scholarship of Teaching and Learning*, edited by Pat Hutchings, 81–93. Carnegie Foundation for the Advancement of Teaching.

Salvatori, Mariolina Rizzi, and Patricia Donahue. 2005. *The Elements (and Pleasures) of Difficulty*. Pearson Longman.

Samuel, Michael Anthony. 2017. "Developing a Syntax for SOTL." *Scholarship of Teaching and Learning in the South* 1 (1): 19–38. https://doi.org/10.36615/sotls.v1i1.11.

Scharff, Lauren, and Claire Hamshire. 2022. "Determining SoTL's Grand Challenges: Advocating for a Broader Endeavor for the Scholarship of Teaching and Learning." In *Going Public Reconsidered: Engaging with the World Beyond Academe through the Scholarship of Teaching and Learning*, edited by Nancy L. Chick and Jennifer C. Friberg, 62–75. Stylus.

Scharff, Lauren, Holly Capocchiano, Nancy Chick, Michelle Eady, Jen Friberg, Diana Gregory, Kara Loy, and Trent Maurer. 2023. "Grand Challenges for SoTL." *International Society for the Scholarship of Teaching and Learning*. https://issotl.com/grand-challenges-for-sotl/.

Scholarship of Teaching and Learning in the South. 2022. "Beyond the Pandemic: Lessons for the Future of SOTL in the Global South (Part One)." *Scholarship of Teaching and Learning in the South* 6 (1). https://doi.org/10.36615/sotls.v6i1.

Scholarship of Teaching and Learning in the South. 2022a. "Beyond the Pandemic: Lessons for the Future of SOTL in the Global South (Part Two)." *Scholarship of Teaching and Learning in the South* 6 (2). https://doi.org/10.36615/sotls.v6i2.

Selvarajan, Shanthni, Sue Chang-Koh, and Lavanya Balachandran. 2022. "Regardless of Role: A Community Engagement Festival as a Unique Space for Differentiated Learning Outcomes for Student Leaders and Participants." *Scholarship of Teaching and Learning in the South* 6 (3): 82–107. https://doi.org/10.36615/sotls.v6i3.277.

Shulman, Lee S. 1993. "Teaching as Community Property: Putting an End to Pedagogical Solitude." *Change* 25 (6): 6–7.

Shulman, Lee S. 1999. "Taking Learning Seriously." *Change* 31 (4): 10–17.

Shulman, Lee. 2001. "From Minsk to Pinsk: Why a Scholarship of Teaching and Learning?" *Journal of the Scholarship of Teaching and Learning* 1 (1): 48–53.

Shulman, Lee S. 2004. *The Wisdom of Practice: Essays on Teaching, Learning, and Learning to Teach*. Jossey-Bass.

Shulman, Lee. 2011. "Feature Essays: The Scholarship of Teaching and Learning: A Personal Account and Reflection." *International Journal for the Scholarship of Teaching and Learning* 5 (1). https://doi.org/10.20429/ijsotl.2011.050130.

Simmons, Nicola, Earle Abrahamson, Jessica M. Deshler, Barbara Kensington-Miller, Karen Manarin, Sue Morón-García, Carolyn Oliver, and Joanna Renc-Roe. 2013. "Conflicts and Configurations in a Liminal Space: SoTL Scholars' Identity

Development." *Teaching & Learning Inquiry* 1 (2): 9–21. https://doi.org/10.20343/teachlearninqu.1.2.9.

Singer, Susan R., Natalie R. Nielsen, and Heidi A. Schweingruber, eds. 2012. *Discipline-Based Education Research: Understanding and Improving Learning in Undergraduate Science and Engineering.* National Academies Press.

Steiner, Hillary H. n.d. "Hopscotch 4-SoTL." Accessed May 31, 2024. https://hopscotchmodel.com/4-sotl/.

Stenfors-Hayes, Terese, Maria Weurlander, Lars-Owe Dahlgren, and Håkan Hult. 2010. "Medical Teachers' Professional Development—Perceived Barriers and Opportunities." *Teaching in Higher Education* 15 (4): 399–408. https://doi.org/10.1080/13562517.2010.493352.

Stovall, Mady, Lissi Hansen, and Michelle van Ryn. 2020. "A Critical Review: Moral Injury in Nurses in the Aftermath of a Patient Safety Incident." *Journal of Nursing Scholarship* 52 (3): 320–328. https://doi.org/10.1111/jnu.12551.

Supiano, Beckie. 2022. "The Redefinition of Rigor." *Chronicle of Higher Education,* March 22. https://www.chronicle.com/article/the-redefinition-of-rigor?sra=true.

Swanson, Holly J., Adelola Ojutiku, and Bryan Dewsbury. 2024. "The Impacts of an Academic Intervention Based in Metacognition on Academic Performance." *Teaching & Learning Inquiry* 12, 1–19. https://doi.org/10.20343/teachlearninqu.12.12.

Sword, Helen. 2019. "The First Person." *Teaching & Learning Inquiry* 7 (1): 182–90. https://doi.org/10.20343/teachlearninqu.7.1.12.

Theobald, Elli J., Mariah J. Hill, Elisa Tran, Sweta Agrawal, E. Nicole Arroyo, Shawn Behling, Nyasha Chambwe, Dianne Laboy Cintrón, Jacob D. Cooper, Gideon Dunster, et al. 2020. "Active Learning Narrows Achievement Gaps for

Underrepresented Students in Undergraduate Science, Technology, Engineering, and Math." *Proceedings of the National Academy of Sciences of the United States of America* 117 (12): 6476–6483. https://doi.org/10.1073/pnas.1916903117.

Thomson, Pat. 2017. "Internationalising a Journal Article." *patter* (blog). https://patthomson.net/2017/10/09/internationalising-a-journal-article/.

Trigwell, Keith. 2013. "Evidence of the Impact of Scholarship of Teaching and Learning Purposes." *Teaching & Learning Inquiry* 1 (1): 95–105. https://doi.org/10.20343/teachlearninqu.1.1.95.

Trigwell, Keith, and Michael Prosser. 1996. "Congruence between Intention and Strategy in University Science Teachers' Approaches to Teaching." *Higher Education* 32, 77–87. https://doi.org/10.1007/BF00139219.

Van Zele, Els, Josephina Lenaerts, and Willem Wieme. 2004. "Improving the Usefulness of Concept Maps as a Research Tool for Science Education." *International Journal of Science Education* 26 (9): 1043–1064. https://doi.org/10.1080/1468181032000158336.

Verschelden, Cia. 2025. *Bandwidth Recovery: Helping Students Reclaim Cognitive Resources Lost to Poverty, Racism, and Social Marginalization.* Routledge.

Wang, Xueli. 2024. *Delivering Promise: Equity-Driven Educational Change and Innovation in Community and Technical Colleges.* Harvard Education Press.

Webb, Andrea S., and Ashley J. Welsh. 2021. "Serendipitous Conversations: The 10-Year Journey in Becoming SoTL Scholars and Educators." *International Journal for Academic Development*, 1–14. https://doi.org/10.1080/1360144X.2021.1964510.

Wenger, Etienne. 2000. "Communities of Practice and Social Learning Systems." *Organization* 7 (2): 225–247. https://doi.org/10.1177/135050840072002.

Wenger-Trayner, Etienne, and Beverly Wenger-Trayner. 2015. "Introduction to Communities of Practice: A Brief Overview of the Concept and Its Uses." Last modified June 2015. https://www.wenger-trayner.com/introduction-to-communities-of-practice/.

Werder, Carmen, and Megan M. Otis, eds. 2010. *Engaging Student Voices in the Study of Teaching and Learning*. Stylus.

Weimer, Maryellen. 2001. "Learning More from the Wisdom of Practice." *New Directions for Teaching and Learning* 86, 45–56. https://doi.org/10.1002/tl.15.

Winkelmes, Mary-Ann. 2023. *TILT Higher Ed: Transparency in Teaching & Learning*. Accessed June 27, 2025. https://tilthighered.com/.

Woo, Tiffany, Roger Ho, Arthur Tang, and Wilson Tam. 2020. "Global Prevalence of Burnout Symptoms among Nurses: A Systematic Review and Meta-analysis." *Journal of Psychiatric Research* 123, 9–20. https://doi.org/10.1016/j.jpsychires.2019.12.015.

"Writing for TLI's Diverse Readers: Principles and Practices." 2020. *Teaching & Learning Inquiry*. Accessed June 27, 2025. https://journalhosting.ucalgary.ca/index.php/TLI/writing-for-diversity.

Yeo, Michelle, and Cherie Woolmer. 2022. "Wrestling the Monster: Novice SoTL Researchers, Ethics, and the Dual Role." In *Ethics and the Scholarship of Teaching and Learning*, 29–42. Springer International Publishing.

Yeo, Michelle, Karen Manarin, and Janice Miller-Young. 2018. "Phenomenology of Surprise in a SoTL Scholars' Program."

Teaching & Learning Inquiry 6 (2): 16–28. https://doi.org/10.20343/teachlearninqu.6.2.3.

Yeo, Michelle, Janice Miller-Young, and Karen Manarin. 2023. *SoTL Research Methodologies: A Guide to Conceptualizing and Conducting the Scholarship of Teaching and Learning*. Routledge.

Yeong, Foong May. 2021. "Using Asynchronous, Online Discussion Forums to Explore How Life Sciences Students Approach an Ill-Structured Problem." *Teaching & Learning Inquiry* 9 (1): 138–60. https://doi.org/10.20343/teachlearninqu.9.1.11.

Yosso, Tara J. 2005. "Whose Culture Has Capital? A Critical Race Theory Discussion of Community Cultural Wealth." *Race, Ethnicity, and Education* 8 (1): 69–91. https://doi.org/10.1080/1361332052000341006.

Zhao, FangFang, Gillian Roehrig, Lorelei Patrick, Chantal Levesque-Bristol, and Sehoya Cotner. 2021. "Using a Self-Determination Theory Approach to Understand Student Perceptions of Inquiry-Based Learning." *Teaching & Learning Inquiry* 9 (2): 1–19. https://doi.org/10.20343/teachlearninqu.9.2.5.

Index

A
academic developers, 5, 6, 31
analysis of SoTL artifacts, 98, 123, 124, 138, 147, 148, 151–164
  principles of systematic SoTL analysis, 154–157
artifact, defined, 137–138
artificial intelligence, 3, 108

B
belief, as entry point to SoTL, 55–56
big tent SoTL, 46–48

C
career stage, 31
citation practices, 3–4, 91, 102–105
collegial self, 33–34
commitments, as entry point to SoTL, 65–67
community of SoTL scholars, 205–221
Conceptual Change/Student-Focused approach to teaching, 17–18
context
  as entry point to SoTL, 57–59
  designing inquiry in, 132–133
curiosity, 49, 127, 198

D
data defined, 135–137
disciplinary self, 28–31
diversity of the field, 46–48, 121–123, 139–140, 210, 211–214

E
entry points, 44–68
ethics, as relational, 107–119
ethics approval, 109–111, 112, 115
evidence, defined, 135–137

G
gaps, as entry point to SoTL, 62–65
Google Scholar, for literature review, 94–96

H

hidden curriculum, 85–87, 90, 107
high-impact educational practices (HIPs), 7, 73

I

implications of SoTL engagement, 188–203
  on scholarly activity, 196–199
  on self, 199–203
  on teaching, 190–196
institutional culture, 20–21, 37–39
institutional environment, 20–21
institutional review board (IRB). *See* ethical approval

L

literature review, 86–106

N

national professional standards frameworks for higher education, 21

O

online education, 233–250
open educational resources (OERs), 97–99, 103

P

peer review, 12–13, 183–185
positionality, 29–31
prior knowledge, as entry point to SoTL, 53–55
problems, as entry point to SoTL, 51–53
public good, 11, 16, 22–23, 40–41, 74, 167
public SoTL, 22–23, 173, 174
  6 Ps of going public with SoTL, 166–174

Q

questions
  five characteristics of SoTL questions, 71–72
  taxonomy of SoTL questions, 75–82
  what if, 76–77
  what is, 75–80, 84, 123–128
  what works, 75–77, 79–82, 83, 116, 128–132

R

reasons to do SoTL, 16–23
reflection
  as a practice, 26–28
  on the profession, 39–40
  on the public good, 40
  on your institutional culture, 37–39
  on your students and their learning, 35–37
  on your teaching, 34–35
  on yourself, 28–34
  prompts, 29–41, 49, 53, 55, 56, 58, 61–62, 64–65, 67

S

scholarship of teaching and learning
  as a space, 46–48
  defined, 2, 10–13
  in translation, 13–14
  origin of, 10–13
  significance of, 12
  versus educational research, 15
  versus discipline-based educational research (DBER), 15
  versus scholarly teaching, 12–13
significant conversations, 33, 171–172, 215

student learning, 18–20, 35–36, 71–72, 127, 131, 136–137, 142–149
students as partners, 19, 113–115, 213–214

T

taxonomy of SoTL questions, 75–84
traces of learning, 135, 138–149

trading zone, 46–48, 121–123, 139–140
transparency, 158–164, 195–196

V

variation, as entry point to SoTL, 60–62

www.ingramcontent.com/pod-product-compliance
Lightning Source LLC
Chambersburg PA
CBHW032213230426
43672CB00011B/2534